974.6
Ken

6515

DATE DUE

6515

Metro Litho
Oak Forest, IL 60452

JAN 1 8 1993			

00453-0

974.6   Kent, Deborah
KEN   America the beautiful.
             Connecticut

AMERICA the BEAUTIFUL
CONNECTICUT

By Deborah Kent

Consultants

Kenneth A. Lester, Ed.D., Education Consultant, Connecticut State Department of Education

Robert L. Hillerich, Ph.D., Bowling Green State University, Bowling Green, Ohio

CHILDRENS PRESS®
CHICAGO

A rural scene near Kent

Project Editor: Joan Downing
Associate Editor: Shari Joffe
Design Director: Margrit Fiddle
Typesetting: Graphic Connections, Inc.
Engraving: Liberty Photoengraving

Library of Congress Cataloging-in-Publication Data

Kent, Deborah.
  America the beautiful. Connecticut / by Deborah
Kent.
    p.   cm.
  Includes index.
  Summary: Introduces the geography, history,
government, economy, industry, culture, historic
sites, and famous people of this northeastern state.
    ISBN 0-516-00453-0
  1. Connecticut—Juvenile literature.
[1. Connecticut.] I. Title.
F94.3.K46   1989   89-17297
974.6—dc20   CIP
                                            AC

A Wesleyan University crew

TABLE OF CONTENTS

Chapter 1
IN THE LAND OF STEADY HABITS

IN THE LAND OF STEADY HABITS

In 1835, a devastating fire swept Manhattan, leaving dozens of square blocks in charred ruins. Most New York insurance companies were overwhelmed with claims, and could not pay their clients for the losses they had suffered. But one insurance company, in Hartford, Connecticut, promptly reimbursed its clients and helped them begin to rebuild their lives. New York's disaster became Connecticut's boon. The insurance companies of Hartford won a reputation for reliability, a reputation that has survived to this day.

The insurance industry is an example of Connecticut's solidity in business enterprises. Connecticut has long been a prosperous state where people work hard and invest carefully. The people of Connecticut have sometimes been characterized as practical, even conservative and predictable. One of the state's nicknames is the Land of Steady Habits.

Yet at the same time, the people of Connecticut have been famous for being innovators. Connecticut framed the New World's first constitution, in 1639. The first cotton gin, the first atomic submarine, and hundreds of other inventions were conceived by the state's daringly creative men and women. American historian Don C. Seitz wrote, "Connecticut, not necessity, is the mother of invention."

These two strands of character—inventiveness and deep-seated practicality—work together to keep Connecticut in balance, a balance it has maintained through a history that spans more than 350 years.

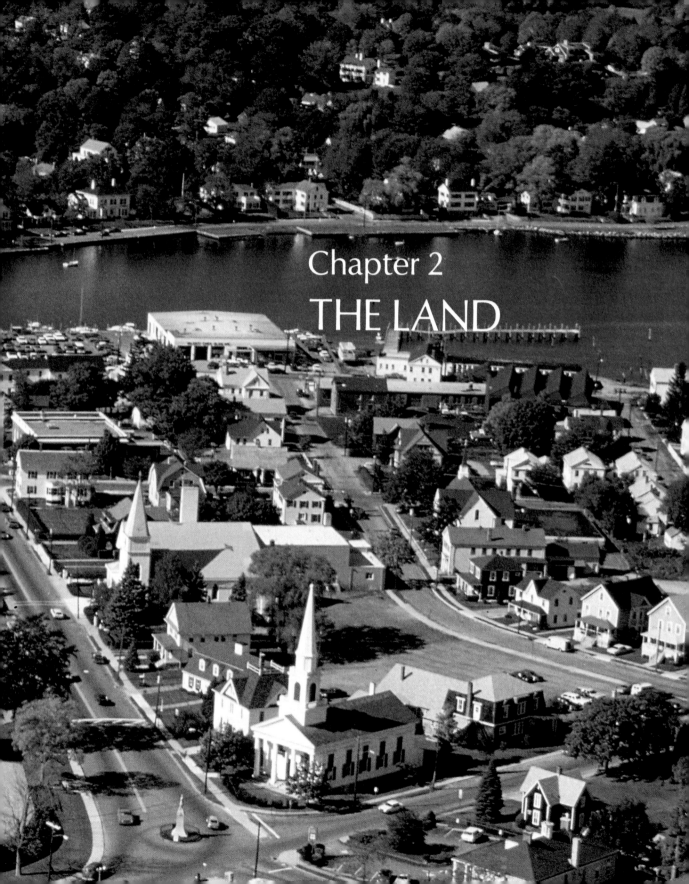

Chapter 2

THE LAND

THE LAND

*I conceded that [Connecticut] had its charms,
but I was still bemused by miles and acres.
The whole of Connecticut wasn't a great deal bigger
than a county in Colorado, where I had grown up.*
—Hal Borland, novelist

GEOGRAPHY AND TOPOGRAPHY

With an area of 5,018 square miles (12,997 square kilometers), Connecticut ranks forty-eighth in size among the fifty states. Only Delaware and Rhode Island are smaller. Fifty-three Connecticuts could fit comfortably into the state of Texas.

Tiny though it is, however, Connecticut offers a delightful variety of landscapes. Its coastline is a vacationer's dream of sandy beaches and hidden coves. Farther inland lies the rich farmland of the Central Valley, cradled by wooded hills to the east and west. Connecticut has teeming industrial cities as well as some of the least-developed countryside in the northeastern United States.

On the map, Connecticut is rectangular in shape with a spur jutting from its southwestern corner. Connecticut is the southernmost of the six states in the New England region. It shares almost straight borders with New York to the west, Massachusetts to the north, and Rhode Island to the east. To the south lies Long Island Sound, a finger of the Atlantic Ocean that stretches between New York's Long Island and the mainland.

A Sharon farm, in the Western New England Upland

The land we know as Connecticut was molded over hundreds of millions of years by the pounding of ancient seas, the action of volcanoes, and the endless erosion of wind and rain. Between twenty thousand and ten thousand years ago, a series of vast glaciers ground their way down from the Arctic to put the finishing touches on the terrain. The glaciers dragged boulders and heaps of earth from farther north and deposited them in Connecticut. Some of this rubble blocked rivers, creating lakes and marshes. Rounded hills of glacial debris, known as drumlins, are still scattered across the state.

LAND REGIONS

Connecticut falls into five land regions: the Taconic Section, the Central Valley, the Western New England Upland, the Eastern New England Upland, and the Coastal Plain.

This ravine is located in the Berkshire Hills, part of the Taconic Section of Connecticut.

The beautiful Taconic Mountains, in the Taconic Section, extend from New York into Connecticut's northwestern corner. On the south slope of Mount Frissell, part of the Taconic Range, is the state's highest point, which is 2,380 feet (725 meters) above sea level.

The Central Valley is a narrow band of lowlands that extends from north to south, nearly dividing the state in half. North of Middletown, the valley is formed by the Connecticut River. South of Middletown, where the river veers into the eastern hills, the valley continues for several more miles to the south. Corn, potatoes, brussels sprouts, tobacco, and many other crops flourish in the rich soil of this region.

On either side of the Central Valley, the land breaks into chains

Connecticut's dwindling salt marshes provide food for such wading birds as the egrets shown here.

of low, wooded hills. The thin, stony soil of these uplands is of little use for farming. In general, the Western Upland has higher elevations than the Eastern Upland.

Connecticut's Coastal Plain is part of a band of lowlands that stretches along most of the nation's Atlantic Coast. In Connecticut, the Coastal Plain is a smooth strip of land from 6 to 16 miles (10 to 26 kilometers) wide, fronting Long Island Sound. With its bays, coves, and offshore islands, Connecticut has 618 miles (994 kilometers) of coastline. Its beaches and state parks are summer playgrounds for families from New York City and other nearby cities. Much of the shoreline has been developed for private residential or commercial use, but environmentalists are working to preserve the remaining salt marshes as wildlife sanctuaries.

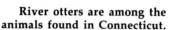
River otters are among the
animals found in Connecticut.

RIVERS AND LAKES

Connecticut's chief waterway, the Connecticut River, rises in
Connecticut Lakes in northern New Hampshire and wanders
south through New Hampshire and Massachusetts. It enters
Connecticut north of Thompsonville and flows south to empty
into Long Island Sound. The Connecticut is navigable by
oceangoing ships as far north as Hartford and by smaller craft as
far north as Holyoke, Massachusetts.

The chief river in western Connecticut is the Housatonic. The
Housatonic enters the state from Massachusetts and is joined at
Shelton and Derby by its main tributary, the Naugatuck. In the
Eastern Upland, the Quinebaug and Shetucket rivers feed into the
Thames River.

Connecticut has more than a thousand lakes, most of them very
small. The largest of these is man-made Lake Candlewood.

Deer are fairly common in the state's forested areas.

Natural lakes in the state include Waramaug, Pocotopaug, Gardner, Bantam, and Twin lakes.

PLANTS AND ANIMALS

About 60 percent of Connecticut's land is covered with forests of ash, beech, birch, hickory, maple, and oak, as well as evergreens such as pine and hemlock. In the spring, Connecticut's state flower, the mountain laurel, cloaks the hills, and dogwoods bloom throughout the state.

White-tailed deer are fairly common in Connecticut's forests. Other animals found in the state include raccoons, opossums, skunks, red foxes, muskrats, minks, otters, woodchucks, gray squirrels, and cottontail rabbits. Many songbirds nest in the state, and gulls, sandpipers, terns, and other shorebirds can be seen along Long Island Sound. Clams and oysters are harvested off the

coast, though the number taken has decreased greatly in recent years.

CLIMATE

"In the spring I have counted one hundred and thirty-six different kinds of weather inside of twenty-four hours," wrote humorist Mark Twain in 1876, after having spent six years in Hartford. He went on to spoof a typical weather forecast: "Probable nor'east to sou'west winds, varying to the southward and westward and eastward and points between; high and low barometer, sweeping round from place to place; probable areas of rain, snow, hail, and drought, succeeded or preceded by earthquakes with thunder and lightning."

Connecticut's weather can, in fact, be varied and uncertain. Every few years tropical hurricanes blow their way as far north as the Connecticut coast. New York's Long Island, however, serves as a barricade to protect the state from some of the worst North Atlantic storms. Blizzards sometimes shut down cities. In the early 1960s and again in 1981, severe droughts destroyed crops and required the rationing of drinking water.

Maples in autumn at Nash's Pond in Westport

Overall, however, Connecticut's climate is relatively mild. January temperatures average 26 degrees Fahrenheit (minus 3.3 degrees Celsius). The average temperature in July is a balmy 71 degrees Fahrenheit (21.6 degrees Celsius), with cool breezes fanning the beaches. The hottest temperature ever recorded in the state was 105 degrees Fahrenheit (40.5 degrees Celsius) at Waterbury on July 22, 1926. On February 16, 1943, the mercury plunged to a record minus 32 degrees Fahrenheit (minus 35.5 degrees Celsius) at Falls Village. Average annual precipitation is about 46 inches (117 centimeters), including about 25 inches (64 centimeters) of snow.

Chapter 3
THE PEOPLE

THE PEOPLE

In 1832, French traveler Alexis de Tocqueville noted that Connecticut gave America "the clock peddler, the schoolmaster, and the senator. The first gives you the time, the second tells you what to do with it, and the third makes your law and civilization."

As in the 1830s, the people of Connecticut are still employed in every walk of life. From factory workers to scholars, they are helping to build American civilization today.

POPULATION

With 3,107,576 people (according to the 1980 census), Connecticut ranks twenty-fifth in population among the states. About 79 percent of Connecticut's people live in urban areas. Tiny as it is, Connecticut is among the most crowded states in the nation, with an average of 619 people for every square mile (239 people per square kilometer) of land. The United States, as a whole, averages a population density of only 67 people per square mile (26 people per square kilometer).

Despite Connecticut's dense population, however, 21 percent of the people in the state live on farms or in small towns. Connecticut possesses some of the most thinly populated regions within an easy drive of New York City. Airline pilots claim that northeastern Connecticut is one of the few dark spots they pass at night between Boston and Washington, D.C.

Connecticut's population is most heavily concentrated in the Central Valley and along the western shore of Long Island Sound. Bridgeport is the state's largest city, with 142,546 people in 1980. Hartford, the state capital, is slightly less populated than Bridgeport; and New Haven, Waterbury, and Stamford each have more than 100,000 people.

Since the 1950s, Connecticut has reflected the national trend toward suburbanization. Bridgeport, Hartford, and other major cities have lost population. But the communities surrounding them are mushrooming so fast that some can barely meet the demand for housing, schools, and other services.

Some towns in Connecticut, especially in Fairfield County in the southwestern corner of the state, are essentially "bedroom communities." Thousands of people from these towns commute every day to jobs in New York City, coming home only to sleep at night. Recently, however, this trend has begun to shift. In the 1970s and 1980s, soaring rents and property values in New York forced many businesses to move to Connecticut and other neighboring states.

WHO LIVES IN CONNECTICUT?

Immigrants from England who had first lived in Massachusetts were the first Europeans to settle in Connecticut. The descendants of these early English settlers came to be known as "Yankees." For generations, the Yankees were Connecticut's dominant ethnic group.

In the middle of the nineteenth century, Irish immigrants flocked to the United States, and thousands of them settled in Connecticut. The following decades brought waves of Poles, Italians, and French Canadians. By about 1870, blacks from the

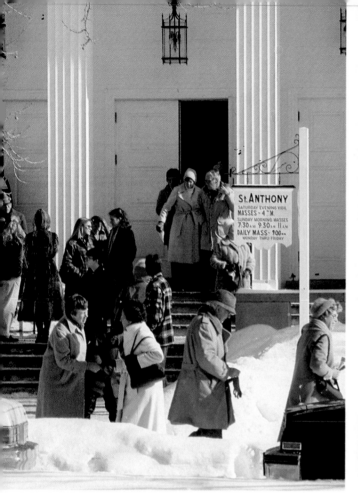

This Roman Catholic Church (left) and an 1829 Congregational
Church (right) are both in Litchfield.

southern states began moving into Connecticut, a migration that
intensified in the first half of the twentieth century.

Today, Connecticut Yankees are only a tiny minority. People of
every ethnic background can be found in the state. Blacks
comprise nearly 7 percent of the population. About 125,000
Hispanics live in Connecticut, most of them Puerto Ricans who
arrived after 1960. Connecticut's Chinese and Southeast Asian
populations are small but rapidly expanding.

Most of Connecticut's early English settlers were devout
Puritans. Puritanism evolved to become the Congregational
church, a Protestant denomination that still has many followers in

Connecticut. Other important Protestant churches in the state include the Episcopal, Presbyterian, Methodist, Lutheran, and Baptist. The Roman Catholic church has more members than any other church in the state. The Jewish population is concentrated in the large cities and in many suburban communities as well.

POLITICS

During the nineteenth century, the Republican party gained a staunch following in Connecticut, and dominated state politics until the 1930s. During the Great Depression, however, Democrats won many key elections in the state. Today, Connecticut's votes are almost equally divided between the two political parties. Since 1956, all but one of the state's governors have been Democrats. Yet the majority of Connecticut voters have supported the Republican candidate in every presidential election from 1972 to 1988.

In general, Connecticut's more affluent citizens favor the Republican party. Political analysts sometimes speak of a "Republican corridor" that stretches from Hartford through Fairfield County. The Democratic party is strongest among the working-class people of Bridgeport and New Haven, and in some parts of eastern Connecticut. Yet there is nothing hard-and-fast about these voting trends.

Like the voters, Connecticut's elected officials do not necessarily adhere to rigid party lines. United States Senator Lowell Weicker, Jr., a Republican who served from 1971 to 1989, championed many causes more often associated with the Democrats. Weicker favored generous spending for education and social services. He also opposed heavy Pentagon spending, despite the fact that military contracts are a mainstay of Connecticut's economy.

Chapter 4
IN THE BEGINNING

IN THE BEGINNING

Long, long ago, or so the legend runs, the Indians near Killingly used to hold feasts at the top of a high mountain. But the Great Spirit grew angry because the people no longer respected the gods. One day, as the Indians were eating and dancing, the mountain shuddered and sank beneath the waters of what is now Loon Lake. Of all the mighty tribe, only one devout old woman survived.

As they retold this tale of annihilation, perhaps the Indians sensed that their way of life was doomed. Early in the 1600s, newcomers reached Connecticut from across the Atlantic Ocean. Their arrival brought devastating change to Connecticut's Indian people.

CONNECTICUT'S FIRST PEOPLE

Only about seven thousand Indians inhabited Connecticut when the Europeans arrived in the seventeenth century. They belonged to the large family of Algonquian-speaking tribes who lived in northeastern North America. Four main Algonquian groups, which were further divided into numerous subgroups, inhabited the land that is now Connecticut. They waged frequent wars among themselves and were never able to unite against their common enemies.

The seven thousand Indians who inhabited Connecticut when the Europeans arrived belonged to Algonquian-speaking groups.

The Matabesecs were a group of tribes who lived in the hills of western Connecticut. Along the Connecticut River lived a loose confederation of tribes called the Sequins. The peaceful Nipmuc people lived in the forests of the northeast. The stronghold of Connecticut's most powerful group, the Pequots, lay in the forests of the southeast. The name *Pequot* translates into English as "destroyer of men." In 1637, shortly after the first European settlements were established, a rebellious Pequot chief named Uncas broke with his tribe and founded a warlike new group, the Mohegans.

The Indians of these tribes hunted game in the forests and fished the coastal waters and rivers. Fish were so plentiful that children could wade into the streams and club them with sticks. The women tended the crops—pumpkins, squash, potatoes, tobacco, and corn. Corn was a staple food that could be roasted, ground into meal, or, perhaps as a special treat, popped over an open fire. Whole villages moved frequently. The Indians did not have the concept that land could be owned. They shared the land communally and used its resources with respect.

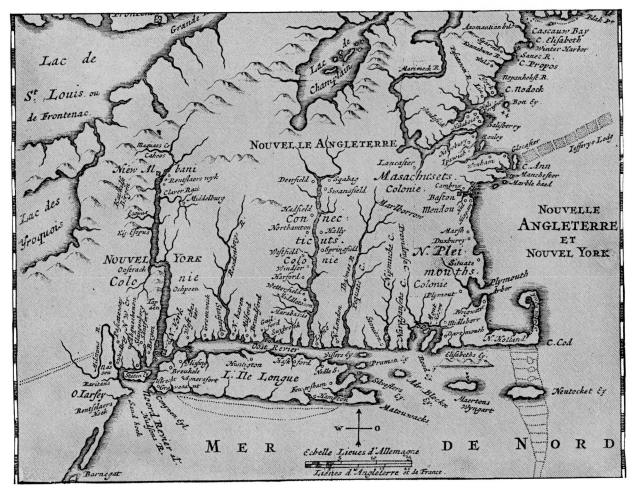

This 1688 French map of New England shows some early place names, including Adriaen Block's Island.

THE COMING OF THE EUROPEANS

In 1614, a Dutch explorer named Adriaen Block sailed his ship the *Restless* into the mouth of the Connecticut River. Fighting the current, he headed upstream as far as present-day Hartford. He may even have reached the rapids at Enfield. Most historians agree that Block and his party were the first Europeans to set foot in Connecticut.

Dutch traders were thrilled by Block's report of forests alive with beavers and other fur-bearing animals. They sailed to the new land and began bartering with the Indians, exchanging kettles, guns, and rum for as many as ten thousand beaver pelts a year. In 1633, the Dutch established a colony on the site of present-day Hartford.

To the north, in the English colony at Massachusetts Bay, people also coveted the rich forests of Connecticut. In 1631, a Sequin chief, eager to make an alliance with the English to strengthen his tribe against enemy tribes, invited the colonies to trade with his people. He also boasted to them about the fertile farmland in the Connecticut Valley. In 1633, an adventurous colonist named John Oldham went to see the valley for himself. He carried back a glowing report of its possibilities for farming and trade, claiming that he had "discovered many very desirable places upon the . . . river fit to receive many hundred inhabitants." In that same year, another Massachusetts colonist, William Holmes, set up a trading post in what is now Windsor.

The next year, Oldham led a small group of followers into the Connecticut wilderness. They cleared land on the banks of the Connecticut River and established a tiny settlement at present-day Wethersfield. More colonists from Massachusetts reached Connecticut in 1635, settling along the river at Windsor and Hartford. In 1636, Hartford, Windsor, and Wethersfield united to form the Connecticut Colony.

A separate colony was established at Quinnipiac (present-day New Haven) in 1638, under the leadership of Reverend John Davenport. Within a few years, the New Haven Colony included rhyming couplets of coastal towns: Milford and Guilford, Stamford and Branford.

At first, most of the Indians welcomed the newcomers as allies against their enemies, the powerful Iroquois. They sold land to the colonists and taught them to grow corn and other crops.

The Connecticut colonists defeated the remaining Pequots in 1637 at the Battle at Fairfield Swamp.

From the outset, however, the Pequots resented white encroachment on their territory. Frequent skirmishes erupted between English traders and Pequot war parties. When John Oldham was killed in 1636 by Indians who were friendly with the Pequots, the colonists blamed the Pequots for his murder and struck back—ineffectively. In the spring of 1637, Captain John Mason led an armed band from Hartford, Windsor, and Wethersfield against the Pequot stronghold at Mystic. Mason was aided by Uncas, the Mohegan chief, who hoped to gain power over his former people.

Mason and his party took the Pequots completely by surprise. They burned the Pequot fort, mercilessly slaying all who tried to escape, including women and children. With more than six hundred dead, the Pequots were crushed forever. Captain Mason wrote, "Thus the Lord was pleased to smite our enemies, and to give us their land for an inheritance."

LIFE IN COLONIAL CONNECTICUT

The Massachusetts Bay Colony had been founded by followers of the Puritan religion. Many Puritans had fled from persecution in England, where the law forbade any but the Anglican church. The Puritans who sailed to Massachusetts hoped that in the New World they could build a society based on their religious beliefs.

The bands of settlers who came to Connecticut's Central Valley brought their strict Puritan doctrine with them from Massachusetts. They believed that human beings were inherently evil and could be saved from sin only through lifelong devotion to God. The Puritans felt that they alone possessed the one true faith, based on their careful study of the Bible and the preachings of their learned ministers.

The Puritans established the Connecticut Colony as a theocracy—a community governed by the church. When the Reverend Thomas Hooker arrived in Hartford from Massachusetts in 1636, he became the colony's political and spiritual leader. He believed that the people should have a larger role in government and should be allowed to elect their leaders. In 1639, Hooker and several other respected ministers drew up the Fundamental Orders, a written code of laws by which the colony would be governed. The Fundamental Orders of 1639 is regarded as the first constitution ever framed in the Western Hemisphere, earning Connecticut another of its nicknames—the Constitution State.

Throughout the colonial period, only members of the Congregational church (as the Puritan church came to be known) had a voice in government. Even among church members, only white male property holders were allowed to vote. A cluster of powerful landowning families, therefore, controlled the colonial legislature.

During the second half of the seventeenth century, dozens of suspected witches were tried and several went to the gallows.

Although the Puritans themselves had suffered from religious persecution, they were less than tolerant of others with differing beliefs. Quakers and Rogerenes (early Seventh-Day Adventists) were driven out of the colony. In 1647, Connecticut became the first New England colony to convict and hang a woman for practicing witchcraft. Over the next fifty years, dozens of suspected witches were tried, and several went to the gallows.

Education was important to the Connecticut Puritans. As early as 1650, a law required every town of fifty families or more to hire a teacher to instruct the children in reading and writing. Parents and teachers demanded strict obedience. Laziness was never permitted. At home, children were contributing members of the family. Boys tended the fields, chopped firewood, and fed the

Connecticut colonists bought such items as cloth, pins and needles, and toys from "Yankee peddlers" who traveled from house to house.

horses, cows, and pigs. Girls helped their mothers with the cooking, washing, and mending, and cared for their younger brothers and sisters.

Most of the colonists made their living as farmers. They planted rye, oats, peas, squash, and turnips. Around Wethersfield, onions became a major crop for export, and the farmers around Windsor grew tobacco. Corn was the colonists' staple food, as it had been for the Indians.

Even in the fertile Connecticut Valley, farming could be a frustrating business. One old saying about the corn crop goes: "One for the bug and one for the crow, one to rot and two to grow."

Most Connecticut families raised their own food and made their own clothing. From shopkeepers in town they purchased such imported goods as molasses, spices, glassware, and gunpowder.

Enterprising "Yankee peddlers" traveled from house to house with ribbon, cloth, pins and needles, toys, and other novelties in their packs.

For peddlers and other travelers, the roads in colonial Connecticut could be a nightmare. On a trip from Boston to New Haven in 1704, a woman named Sarah Kemble Knight wrote in her journal: "The roads all along this way are very bad, encumbered with rocks and mountainous passages which were very disagreeable to my tired carcass. In going over a bridge under which the river runs very swift, my horse stumbled and very narrowly escaped falling into the water, which extremely frightened me. But through God's goodness I met with no harm."

When Thomas Hooker arrived in 1636, he presided over a struggling colony of some eight hundred people. By 1700, the population of Connecticut had soared to thirty thousand. Towns flourished in the Central Valley and along the coast. As the population grew, families moved into the highlands in search of more farmland. Despite the harshness of life, Connecticut was thriving.

THE SEEDS OF REVOLUTION

In 1662, King Charles II of England granted Connecticut a charter that made it almost independent of the mother country. Connecticut was even permitted to elect its own governor, while the other English colonies were ruled by appointed officials. The king gave the Connecticut Colony a strip of land that included the New Haven Colony. Though New Haven objected at first, the two colonies united in 1665.

Connecticut's independence was challenged twenty-five years later, when the royal governor of New York, Sir Edmund Andros,

When Sir Edmund Andros ordered the colonial legislature to hand over the Connecticut Charter, the charter was hidden in the hollow of an oak tree, which was later called the Charter Oak.

attempted to gain control over its eastern neighbor. In October 1687, Andros arrived in Hartford and ordered the colonial legislature to hand over the king's charter at once. According to legend, one of the assemblymen blew out the lamps that lighted the room. Under cover of darkness, another conspirator dashed away with the precious charter and hid it in a hollow oak tree, which was later called the Charter Oak. There the charter remained until Andros no longer posed a threat.

For nearly eighty more years, Connecticut acted almost as an independent republic. Towns held regular town meetings, electing officials and making laws without a thought for British authority. In the meantime, however, the French and Indian War (1756-1763) and a series of costly wars in Europe had driven England into debt. In desperate need of revenue, the English Parliament levied new taxes on the American colonies.

In 1765, Parliament passed the Stamp Act, which required that
licenses, newspapers, legal documents, and even playing cards
carry a stamp sold by the British government. In Connecticut, the
news aroused a thunder of protest, especially in the eastern and
coastal villages and towns. Yet, Governor Thomas Fitch agreed to
comply with the act, and a New Haven lawyer named Jared
Ingersoll accepted the position of stamp distributor.

In Milford, mobs burned bundles of stamped documents. In
New London and Norwich, the townspeople denounced Ingersoll

The Sons of Liberty, a patriotic society formed to protest the Stamp Act, soon grew into a movement for American independence.

as a traitor and hanged him in effigy. In Lebanon, Ingersoll's effigy was tried, convicted, dragged through the streets, and burned before a cheering crowd.

With feelings running so high, Eliphalet Dyer of Windham and Jonathan Trumbull of Lebanon formed a patriotic society called the Sons of Liberty, which quickly gathered members in Connecticut and several other colonies. In one written statement, the Sons of Liberty declared, "We will oppose the [Stamp Act] to the last extremity, even to take the field."

In September 1765, five hundred Sons of Liberty waylaid Ingersoll at Wethersfield and forced him to resign as stamp distributor. Perhaps relieved to be out of the controversial position, Ingersoll threw his hat in the air and gave three cheers for liberty and prosperity.

The opposition of the American colonists forced the British to repeal the Stamp Act in 1766. But the following year, Parliament approved a new set of taxes under the Townshend Acts. Throughout the colonies, voices rose in fresh protest. The people of Connecticut joined Massachusetts and several other colonies in a boycott of British goods until most of the Townshend Acts were repealed in 1770.

Still, tension mounted between the British government and the American colonies. In Connecticut, some patriots vented their anger on the Tories—colonists who remained loyal to the mother country. They drove many Tories out of the colony, confiscating their land and belongings. One Tory, Reverend Samuel Peters of Hebron, wrote, "For my telling the church people not to take up arms, the Sons of Liberty have destroyed my windows, [and] rent my clothes. . . . Treason is common and robbery is their daily diversion. The Lord deliver us from anarchy!"

CONNECTICUT AT WAR

Hostility flared into war before dawn on April 19, 1775, when British troops and colonial militia exchanged gunfire at Lexington and Concord in Massachusetts. At ten o'clock in the morning, a messenger set out from Massachusetts to spread the news. Riding tirelessly for two days and nights, the messenger alerted the farmers and villagers across Connecticut that the time had come to bear arms.

Within days, 3,600 eager militiamen marched north to join the patriots in Boston. One young soldier, Amos Wadsworth of Farmington, wrote to his brother, "If I must lose my life in the defense of my country, the sacrifice will be but small in proportion to the loss of the liberties and privileges . . . of this

Before being hanged by the British, Nathan Hale's last words were: "I only regret that I have but one life to lose for my country."

extensive continent. Better to die a free man than to live a slave."

Meanwhile, in Philadelphia, delegates from each of the colonies were discussing strategies at the Continental Congress. They determined to sever all ties with the British government forever. On July 4, 1776, four representatives from Connecticut were among the signers of the Declaration of Independence.

During the American Revolution, tiny Connecticut produced more than its share of heroes. General Israel Putnam is sometimes called Connecticut's George Washington. Legend claims that he joined the militia the instant he heard that war was declared, leaving his plow standing in the field. Ethan Allen of Litchfield led in the capture of Fort Ticonderoga without losing a single man. And Nathan Hale, a young schoolmaster from Coventry, served as a spy for General Washington early in the war. He was captured by the British and sentenced to be hanged. As he stood on the gallows platform, Hale uttered his eloquent last words: "I only regret that I have but one life to lose for my country."

Turncoat Benedict Arnold led the devastating British attack on Fort Trumbull, at New London.

Jonathan Trumbull, of the Sons of Liberty, served as governor throughout the war. He was sixty-five years old in 1775, but he worked ceaselessly for the American cause during the long war years. From his war office in Lebanon, he organized a highly efficient system for distributing provisions to the troops. In the winter of 1778, he arranged for several herds of cattle to be driven from Hartford to Valley Forge, Pennsylvania, to feed Washington's starving Continental army. Under Trumbull's leadership, Connecticut also furnished powder, guns, cannons, and ships for the war effort.

Red-coated British troops attacked Connecticut several times in the course of the war. In April 1777, the British burned valuable

Continental army supplies stored at Danbury. In February 1779, Israel Putnam drove off British forces when they attacked the saltworks at Greenwich. A few months later, British troops swept through New Haven, Fairfield, and Norwalk, burning and looting as they went. But the bloodiest battle on Connecticut soil was the British assault on New London and Groton.

Two Continental forts, Fort Trumbull and Fort Griswold, guarded the mouth of the Thames River. In September 1781, Benedict Arnold, the newly appointed British general, led 2,000 men in the assault on Fort Trumbull, at New London, which fell quickly under the attack. Resistance was fiercer at Fort Griswold, near Groton, where for a time 150 Americans held off 800 British troops. Though the Americans inflicted heavy casualties, the fort finally fell before a British bayonet charge. The British killed more than 80 Americans, including many wounded men, as they tried to surrender.

The defeats at New London and Groton were especially grievous to the people of Connecticut because Benedict Arnold was one of their native sons. At the start of the war, Arnold had served the Continental army as one of its most gifted generals. But he quarreled with fellow officers and fell into financial debt. Finally, for a sum of six thousand pounds, he accepted an appointment as brigadier general in the British Provincial army. History salutes Putnam, Allen, Hale, and Trumbull as heroes, but Benedict Arnold is remembered to this day as a traitor to his country.

The British surrendered at Yorktown, Virginia, in 1781. The American cause had triumphed at last. Exultant, Jonathan Trumbull wrote to the Continental Congress, "Suffer me to congratulate you on this great event . . . [which] claims our utmost gratitude and love to the Supreme Disposer of all events."

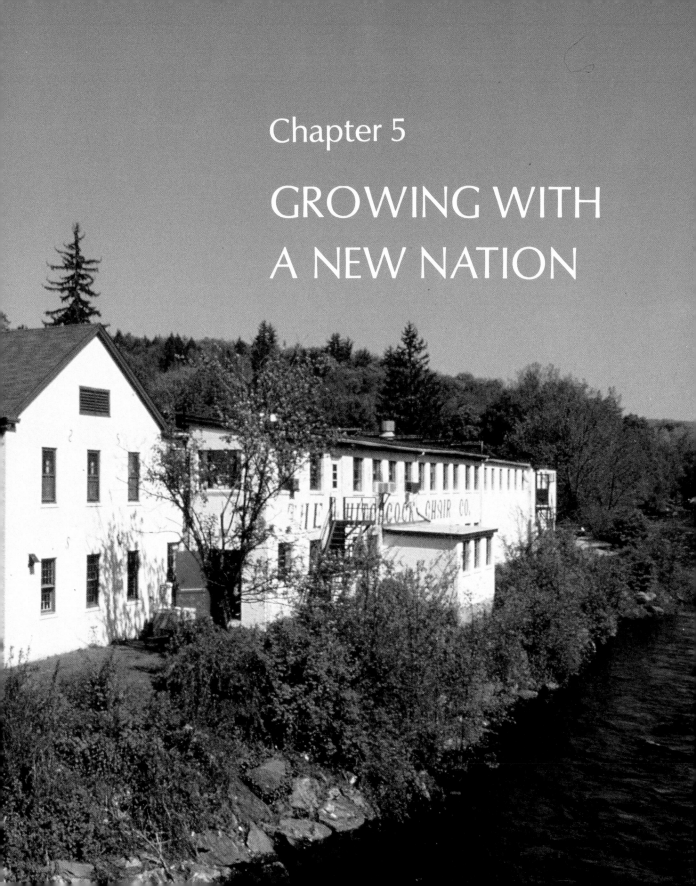

Chapter 5

GROWING WITH
A NEW NATION

GROWING WITH A NEW NATION

Ere death invades and night's dark curtain falls,
Through roaring realms the voice of Union calls:
"O, you," she calls, "attend the warning cry:
We live united, or divided die."
— The *New Haven Gazette*, 1786

These lines urged the former colonies to join forces under a strong centralized government. But for a long time, many people in Connecticut were reluctant to exchange their independence for participation in the new nation.

BECOMING AMERICAN

In the spring and summer of 1787, delegates from each of the thirteen former colonies met in Philadelphia to draw up a constitution for governing their new nation. Until that time, the thirteen states had a weak form of government under the Articles of Confederation. At the Constitutional Convention, in 1787, representatives from the small states worried that the larger states would dominate the central government. At last, the Connecticut delegates, working with those from several other small states, arrived at a compromise. The Great Compromise (sometimes called the Connecticut Compromise) permitted each state, regardless of its size, to send two senators to the upper house of Congress. Representatives would be elected to the lower house on the basis of population. On January 9, 1788, Connecticut became the new nation's fifth state when it ratified the new Constitution of the United States.

For over a century, the people of Connecticut had made their own laws and had elected their own officials, looking only to God as their higher authority. Some resented interference from the new federal government almost as much as they had objected to British taxes.

An important test of the federal government's strength came in the early 1800s, when the United States and Great Britain struggled to determine which nation would rule on the high seas. After a series of clashes, the conflict exploded into war in 1812. Overseas trade was of little importance to Connecticut at that time. Most people in Connecticut saw the war as the concoction of Virginia-born President James Madison. Connecticut refused to send its militia out of the state to serve in "Mr. Madison's War."

In August 1814, a fleet of British warships anchored off Stonington. Commander Thomas M. Hardy sent the townspeople a message, warning them to leave within an hour if they wished to remain safe. With the war on their doorstep, the people chose to resist. Summoning the militia, they repulsed Hardy's landing parties. British cannon fire battered the town, but only one Stonington man was killed. Later, poet Philip Freneau boasted:

> It cost the king ten thousand pounds
> To have a dash at Stonington.

Dissatisfaction with the federal government blossomed in December 1814, when delegates from Connecticut and four other New England states met at the State House in Hartford. The Hartford Convention recommended a series of amendments to the Constitution. Sponsors of the amendments hoped to protect the interests of the New England states. The delegates proposed that

In 1814, New England's dissatisfaction with the federal government led to the Hartford Convention, which met at the State House (above) to recommend a series of constitutional amendments.

individual states, and not the central government, should control defense. To break what they felt was Virginia's hold over the government, they declared that no single state should be allowed to send two successive presidents to the White House.

In the meantime, the rest of the country celebrated the end of the War of 1812 and America's victory over the British. Few people took the recommendations of the Hartford Convention seriously, and even some Connecticut citizens felt the convention had been a mistake. One opponent called it "that foulest stain on our state escutcheon, an imperishable monument of infamy."

PEOPLING A NATION

During the colonial era and in the years after the Revolutionary War, Connecticut families tended to be large. It was common for a

During the late eighteenth century and the first half of the
nineteenth century, thousands of Connecticut families migrated
westward in search of more room and richer farmland.

woman to bear six, eight, or even ten children. If she died, often
from overwork, her husband would usually marry again, and his
second wife might bring five or six more children into the world.
One woman from Windsor, who died in 1768 at the age of eighty-
eight, left behind 10 children, 75 grandchildren, 232 great-
grandchildren, and 19 great-great-grandchildren—a total of 336
living descendants.

The swelling population put a severe strain on Connecticut's
resources. The fertile Central Valley was soon crowded with
farms. More and more families pushed into the uplands, where
the stony soil mocked their most determined efforts.

Spurred by the dream of richer farmland, thousands of families
left Connecticut for less-populated regions. The 1780s saw an
extensive migration north into Vermont and upstate New York.
Another wave of migrants swept into northern Ohio. Until 1795,

Connecticut claimed much of the land along Lake Erie's southern shore, a legacy of the Royal Charter of 1662. The state government awarded portions of this land, known as the Western Reserve, to the people of Danbury, Fairfield, New London, and other towns whose property had been destroyed by the British during the Revolutionary War.

The migrations continued all through the first half of the nineteenth century. Men and women from Connecticut bought land in Michigan, Wisconsin, and Minnesota. Later, they flocked to the plains of Kansas and Nebraska, and followed their dreams to the California goldfields. One eyewitness recalled the spectacle of families on the move: "A sort of stampede took place from cold, desolate, worn-out New England. Some persons went in covered wagons, frequently a family consisting of father, mother, and nine small children . . . some on foot and some crowded together under the cover with kettles, gridirons, featherbeds, crockery, and the family Bible."

The family Bible was indispensable. Wherever they went, the Connecticut farmers carried their deep-rooted Puritan beliefs in hard work and a stern, implacable God. Used to the heartbreak of farming back home, they were well equipped for the hardships of pioneer life.

In spite of the Great Compromise, it could have been argued that tiny Connecticut exerted more than its share of influence in the federal government. By 1831, one-third of the seats in the United States Senate and one-fourth of those in the House of Representatives were filled by men born in Connecticut who had resettled elsewhere. Whether they spoke for Wisconsin or Kansas, they championed many of the principles they had learned to value back home. And one cause that the people of Connecticut were willing to fight for was the abolition of slavery.

Connecticut citizens went to court to help slaves from the Spanish ship *Amistad* win the right to be returned to Africa.

PRESERVING THE UNION

One morning in 1839, fishermen sighted a strange ship drifting aimlessly off Montauk Point, in Long Island Sound. The vessel proved to be a Spanish slave ship, the *Amistad*, which had careened far off course during a bloody slave revolt on board. Ironically, *amistad* is a Spanish word meaning friendship.

The *Amistad* finally landed in Connecticut, and the surviving slaves demanded to return to Africa. Horrified by what these people had suffered, a group of Connecticut citizens raised money and hired leading lawyers to plead their cases. The Connecticut courts ruled in the Africans' favor, and the United States Supreme Court upheld the decision. At last, thirty-five black men, women, and children sailed back to their homeland.

Most of Connecticut's leading families had owned slaves during the colonial period. But the years after the Revolutionary War brought a gradual end to slavery in the state. After March 1, 1784, all children born into slavery were freed when they reached the age of twenty-five. In 1848, the last twenty slaves in Connecticut were given their freedom.

In the southern states, however, slavery had become more crucial than ever to the economy. In 1793, a brilliant Yale graduate named Eli Whitney invented a machine called the cotton gin, which separated the cotton seeds from the valuable cotton fiber far faster than many workers could do the job by hand. The cotton gin led to a tremendous surge in cotton as a cash crop in the South. But the cotton plantations depended heavily on slaves to tend and harvest the crop.

During the 1830s and 1840s, a powerful movement for the total abolition of slavery arose in Connecticut and in many other northern states. Abolitionists argued passionately that slavery was evil, a vile sin in the eyes of God. Through a secret system called the Underground Railroad, many Connecticut men and women aided slaves who were running away from masters in the South. They sheltered the runaways in barns and attics, or transported them in wagons loaded with hay, helping them cross the state safely on their journey to Canada and freedom.

Despite such antislavery feelings, however, Connecticut's black citizens were not entitled to vote. Some whites in the state did not even think black children should receive a quality education. When a young teacher named Prudence Crandall opened a private academy for black girls in Canterbury in 1833, the townspeople

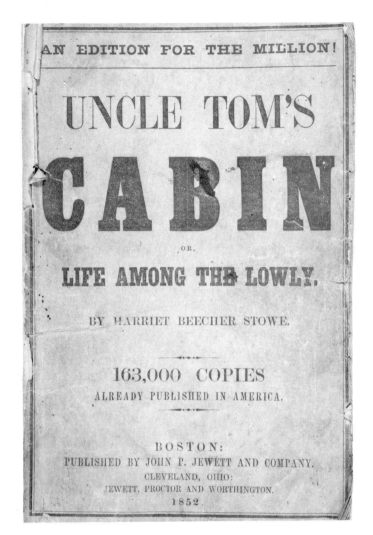

Among the many Connecticut citizens who opposed slavery were Prudence Crandall (above), who opened a school for black girls in 1833, and Harriet Beecher Stowe, who published *Uncle Tom's Cabin* (left), a gripping novel about the evils of slavery.

were outraged. After months of threats and taunts, a mob attacked the school, smashing all of its windows. Crandall was forced to give up, fearing for the safety of her pupils.

In 1852, Harriet Beecher Stowe of Litchfield published a gripping novel about the evils of slavery. *Uncle Tom's Cabin* stirred the consciences of thousands of northerners. In the years that followed, a chasm widened between the free North and the slaveholding South. At last, in 1861, the southern states broke away to form their own nation, the Confederate States of America, launching a long and bloody civil war.

During the Civil War, northern factories produced goods for the Union war effort.

Three days after President Abraham Lincoln declared war in 1861, Connecticut mustered its first regiment of volunteers. Governor William Buckingham worked tirelessly among civilians to organize support for the war effort. Towns sent food and blankets to the men at the front. Factories in Colchester and Naugatuck outfitted the troops with rubber boots and ponchos. New Haven carriage companies began making military transport wagons. Hartford, New Haven, and Middletown factories turned out rifles and revolvers; and in Enfield, the Hazard Powder Company produced 12 tons (11 metric tons) of gunpowder a day.

After two years of fighting and some disastrous Union defeats, however, Connecticut lost much of its enthusiasm for the war. People grew to resent the draft, which took young men from their families, often to die on faraway battlefields. In 1863, Thomas Hart Seymour, a Peace Democrat, ran for governor against Republican William Buckingham. Seymour claimed that the notion of saving the Union through violence was "a monstrous fallacy." Buckingham warned that Seymour would undermine the state's entire war effort. Though Seymour gained many supporters, Buckingham was reelected. Connecticut continued to pour its energies into saving the Union.

By the end of the war, fifty-five thousand Connecticut men had served in the Union army and navy. Of these, a staggering twenty thousand were killed or wounded. But when the terrible struggle was over, the Union had been preserved.

MADE IN CONNECTICUT

While thousands of people abandoned Connecticut in the early 1800s, those who stayed at home did not sit idle. Farmland was limited, but there seemed no limit to the ingenuity of the Connecticut Yankees when they put their minds to a problem.

The growth of the cotton industry in the South before the Civil War, due in part to Eli Whitney's cotton gin, had spurred the development of mills in Connecticut to turn raw cotton into finished cloth. In the early 1800s, hundreds of Connecticut residents had found work in cotton mills at Manchester, Vernon, Pomfret, and Jewett City. The wool industry also boomed in the state after the introduction of merino sheep from Scotland. In 1806, a fully planned industrial community opened around the woolen mills at present-day Seymour.

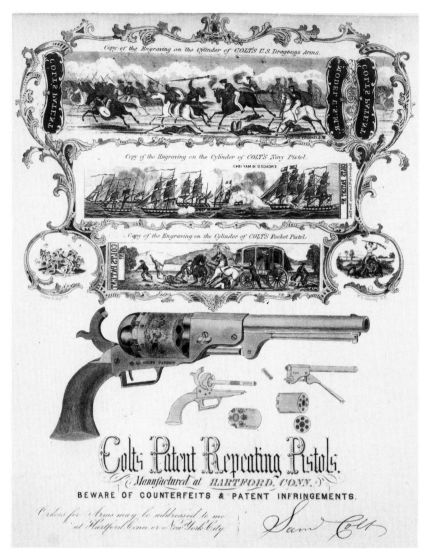

Competitors had cheated Eli Whitney out of most of the profits from the cotton gin. He earned more money, however, if less renown, through his work in the manufacture of firearms. For centuries, guns had been made individually by skilled gunmakers, and no two weapons were exactly alike. Whitney standardized gun parts and manufactured them on a large scale. Parts from one of his guns were interchangeable with parts from any other. If part of one rifle malfunctioned, it could simply be replaced.

In 1798, Whitney put his principles of mass production to work in his firearms factory in Hamden. Other gun manufacturers

The firearms industry became a mainstay of Connecticut's economy, and factories produced cartridges (left) and weapons that helped win the Civil War and conquer the West.

quickly copied his methods. The firearms industry became a mainstay of Connecticut's economy, with such major companies as Colt, Winchester, and Parker turning out the weapons that helped win the Civil War and conquer the American West.

Eli Whitney was only one of a regiment of Connecticut inventors, each of whom added to the state's industrial power. Eli Terry applied Whitney's mass-production techniques to clock making, turning out timepieces that were both attractive and accurate. Working from his home laboratory in Naugatuck, Charles Goodyear developed the vulcanization process for turning

Boedie

The Discovery of the Vulcanization of Rubber by Charles Goodyear 1839

Among Connecticut inventions of the 1800s were vulcanized rubber, developed by Charles Goodyear in his home laboratory (right), and a machine that mass produced pins, made by John I. Howe (above).

raw rubber into the versatile material we know today. In 1832, John I. Howe built a machine for mass-producing pins, which had previously been shaped by hand. J. B. Williams of Glastonbury invented the world's first shaving soap in 1840, and in 1861, Linus Yale developed the cylinder lock.

The westward migration of Connecticut Yankees left the state's population depleted at a time when more and more hands were needed to work in the new mills and factories. Most of the new labor force came from Europe. In the 1840s, a terrible famine swept Ireland, driving hundreds of thousands of people to seek refuge in the United States. Thousands of Irish Catholic immigrants settled in Connecticut. New waves of immigrants poured into the state during the decades after the Civil War. They brought their customs and languages from Poland, Italy, and Quebec.

Many of Connecticut's Italian immigrants took classes in the English language.

With the new immigrant population, the tradition of hard work endured in Connecticut. In factories across the state, from Willimantic to New Haven, immigrant workers toiled from sunrise to dark, making thousands of products that the nation craved. As the nineteenth century drew to a close, Connecticut stood at the forefront of American manufacturing.

In 1902, a Connecticut man named William A. Countryman took a job in Washington, D.C. Perhaps he felt homesick at first, but he soon found traces of his native state all around him. "At my boarding-house I find the plated ware to be of Connecticut manufacture," he wrote in delight. "At the office I write with a Connecticut pen, and when I need an official envelope, I find that the original package from which I take it bears a Connecticut mark. . . . Do I want a button? Made in Connecticut. Hand me a pin. The box tells me it is from Waterbury, Connecticut, USA. That automobile rushing by came from Connecticut, that bicycle, these tires, these . . . doorbells . . . typewriters on every side, all from our little state. . . . And last, let me say that where my trousers are put away at night they go onto a hanger of the best kind, made in Connecticut."

Chapter 6
THE TWENTIETH CENTURY

THE TWENTIETH CENTURY

On October 12, 1935, a spectacular parade wound its way through the streets of Hartford. Costumed men and women on elaborate floats portrayed dramatic moments in Connecticut's history. The parade culminated Connecticut's tercentenary festival—a gala three-hundredth birthday party celebrated with pageants and historical exhibits all across the state.

Connecticut had grown from three tiny villages to a teeming industrial state, the home of about one and a half million people. Yet as it looked back over past struggles and triumphs, Connecticut faced the new challenges of the twentieth century.

WAR AND POLITICS

In 1914, deep-rooted tensions among the nations of Europe erupted into World War I. France and Great Britain contracted with Colt, Remington, and other Connecticut firearms companies, which rushed to assemble weapons for shipment overseas. When the United States entered the conflict in 1917, the arms plants redoubled their efforts. About 20 percent of the rifles, 50 percent of the cartridges, and nearly all of the bayonets used by American soldiers came from Connecticut factories. Other companies turned from the manufacture of civilian goods to the manufacture of military supplies. A silk firm in Manchester made parachutes instead of stockings. Clothing companies in Middletown turned out holsters and haversacks, and the hatmakers of Danbury stitched together caps for military uniforms. Thousands of poor blacks from the southern states moved to Connecticut and took jobs in the state's war plants. Black people continued to migrate into the state for the next twenty years.

When peace returned, Connecticut's economy entered a period of adjustment. War plants laid off thousands of workers. Some textile mills left the state for the South, where wages were lower. But new industries quickly made up for the jobs that were lost. As cars became more popular, Bridgeport began to produce gear shifts, tire valves, and other auto parts. Hartford plants built airplane engines. Other companies in the state responded to the needs of the growing electrical industries, turning out cable, motors, and light sockets. Connecticut's economy boomed, swept along on a national tide of prosperity.

During the 1920s, the Republican party controlled Connecticut, and the reins of the Republican party rested in the hands of J. Henry Roraback. Roraback grew up in North Canaan. He was too poor to attend college, so he studied law on his own while he taught in a country school. In 1910, Roraback became head of Connecticut's Republican Central Committee, a position he held for the next twenty-seven years. He never ran for public office, but worked ceaselessly behind the scenes, supporting candidates and pushing bills through the legislature. Roraback was a dedicated champion of corporate interests in the state. He once said that "good business is good politics; good politics is good business."

DEPRESSION AND RECOVERY

"We in America today are nearer to the final triumph over poverty than ever before in the history of any land," declared

President Herbert Hoover in 1928. Events of the next few years proved the president tragically wrong. By the early 1930s, the United States was plunged into a disastrous economic depression. All across the country, banks closed, factories shut down, and millions of people lost their jobs.

By 1932, about 22 percent of Connecticut's work force was unemployed. In Willimantic and other textile towns, the figure rose as high as 50 percent. Ragged and desperate, a band of "hunger marchers" surrounded the state capitol in Hartford, petitioning the governor for relief.

The Democratic governor, Wilbur L. Cross, was deeply sympathetic to the needs of the unemployed, the ill, and the elderly in Connecticut. When Cross first ran for office in 1930, he challenged not only the Republican candidate, but the whole "political machine" that Roraback had built. A former professor of English at Yale, Cross had grown up on a farm near Mansfield, and his campaign speeches appealed to the earthy humor of the state's rural people. In one speech, he claimed that Roraback was like an old hen that had been "settin' on rotten eggs for fifteen years without hatching out any chickens."

Cross occupied the governor's mansion until 1939, and saw Connecticut through the worst of the Great Depression. He enacted an old-age pension, outlawed work for children under sixteen, and closed brutal sweatshops where immigrant workers earned as little as three dollars a week. He sponsored generous state grants to aid the unemployed.

Even more help came from the federal government, through a series of programs under President Franklin D. Roosevelt's "New Deal." Between 1933 and 1936, about fifteen thousand young Connecticut men worked for the Civilian Conservation Corps (CCC), building bridges, planting trees, and fighting forest fires.

The hurricane that slammed into the Connecticut coast in 1938 was the deadliest hurricane ever to hit New England.

Millions of dollars in unemployment relief fed and clothed families in need.

As though the sagging economy weren't bad enough, the people of Connecticut had to contend with the cruel whims of the weather. In March 1936, the Connecticut River rose to record heights after several days of torrential rain. Floodwaters rushed over Hartford's east side, turning city streets into canals. The flood claimed many lives and destroyed property estimated at $24 million in value. In 1938, a vicious hurricane slammed into Connecticut's coast, taking residents utterly by surprise. The storm swept homes into the sea, tore away great chunks of land, and took eighty-five lives.

During World War II, the Colt Arms Factory in Hartford geared up for the war effort, producing weapons such as machine guns.

The United States finally emerged from the depression with the outbreak of World War II. Once more, Connecticut's factories went into high gear. The state received more than $8 billion in federal contracts to produce ships, communications equipment, and weapons. About seventy-five submarines were built at Groton. Plants in New Britain made commando knives and gun mounts.

CHANGES AND CHALLENGES

In the decades after World War II, Connecticut followed the national tendency toward suburbanization. Middle-class families abandoned Hartford, New Haven, Bridgeport, and other cities for the green lawns and clearer skies of outlying communities. More and more New Yorkers bought homes in Fairfield County and commuted to their offices in Manhattan.

In the 1960s and early 1970s, riots flared in Connecticut cities such as New Haven (above), Hartford, Bridgeport, and Middletown.

The flight of middle-class residents left the cities poorer and more desolate than ever before. Buildings crumbled, and crime rose. Children studied in decaying, ill-equipped schools. By the 1960s, the people of the inner cities, most of whom were black or Hispanic, had little chance to improve their lives.

In New Haven, Mayor Richard Lee determined to reverse the trend. During his seventeen years in office, from 1953 to 1970, Lee turned his boundless energy and imagination to revitalizing the city. He leveled empty warehouses and factories and replaced them with gleaming high-rise apartments and office buildings. His Chapel Square Mall lured suburban shoppers back downtown. During the Lee era, New Haven received more than $110 million in federal money for urban renewal. Looking back, Lee recalled proudly, "We would dream, and we did, and when we succeeded, we succeeded sometimes beyond our fondest expectations."

In 1981, Thirman Milner was elected mayor of Hartford, becoming the first black mayor of a New England City.

Urban renewal programs in New Haven, Hartford, and other cities restored theaters, opened shopping plazas, and created middle- and upper-income housing. But they often overlooked the desperate needs of the poor. During the long, hot summer of 1967, the thwarted dreams of the inner cities exploded in a series of destructive riots. In Bridgeport, Middletown, New Britain, and New London, teenagers smashed windows and looted stores. The worst riots flared in Hartford's poverty-ravaged North End. Surveying the wreckage, reporters compared the area to a battlefield.

Gradually, in the years after the riots, the blacks and Hispanics of Connecticut's inner cities gained greater political power. With a growing voice in city government, they fought to improve low-income housing, health services, and public schools. In 1981, Hartford became the first New England city to elect a black mayor, Thirman Milner.

By the 1980s, Connecticut had the third-highest per-capita income in the United States, exceeded only by Alaska and Washington, D.C. But Connecticut also claimed the nation's highest cost of living. Energy and housing costs were among the steepest in the country. A house in Hartford cost twice as much as a similar house in Chicago or Cincinnati. Under those circumstances, it was difficult for low-income families to survive. A 1988 study found that Connecticut had more homeless people, per capita, than any other state.

When the people of Connecticut elected Ella Grasso to serve as their governor in 1974, she became the first woman in the United States to win a governorship in her own right. (A few other women, such as Lurleen Wallace of Alabama, had become governor by succeeding their husbands or by appointment.) In her campaign, Grasso pledged that she would never impose a state income tax, a promise she kept throughout her six years in office.

By the late 1980s, however, some political leaders argued that Connecticut's sales tax burdened poor people unfairly. They argued that a state income tax would draw more revenue from wealthier residents and could provide funds for badly needed social programs. Yet the notion of a state income tax has remained unpopular with most Connecticut voters.

SAVING THE LAND

In March 1988, a seventy-year-old Ledyard woman donated 234 acres (94.6 hectares) of shorefront land near the mouth of the Thames River as a wildlife preserve. The land had been in her family for generations and was valued at over $1 million. "Developers were calling me all the time, offering any price I wanted," she told reporters. "But I stood up to them. I never really

In 1974, Ella Grasso was elected governor of Connecticut, becoming the first woman in the United States to win a governorship in her own right.

felt I owned the land . . . I felt I was just someone taking care of it. Now I'm giving it back for someone else to conserve."

How Connecticut's limited land should be used became a controversial issue during the 1970s and 1980s. Environmentalists estimate that Connecticut loses 20,000 acres (8,094 hectares) of unspoiled land to commercial development each year. More wetlands are drained annually in Connecticut than in all of the other New England states combined. Forests are razed to make room for shopping malls, and condominiums sprout along once-lonely beaches.

To Connecticut's Puritan settlers, the wilderness was an enemy to be conquered. Today, more and more people in Connecticut regard the state's remaining wild places as a priceless resource. Connecticut still offers urban dwellers the opportunity to explore wooded streams, forest trails, and hidden coves where ospreys nest. In such a tiny state, these undeveloped areas are never more than a few miles away, enhancing the quality of life for everyone.

As the twentieth century draws to a close, Connecticut struggles to balance the demand for housing and jobs with the need to protect its natural landscape. People like the woman from Ledyard are pointing the way, looking beyond personal gain to preserve the land as a gift for future generations.

Chapter 7
GOVERNMENT AND THE ECONOMY

GOVERNMENT AND THE ECONOMY

GOVERNMENT

Connecticut's current state constitution was ratified in 1965. The constitution divides the state government into three branches, much like the three branches of the federal government in Washington, D.C. The legislative branch enacts the laws. The judicial branch interprets the laws, and the executive branch ensures that the laws are carried out.

The legislature, known as the General Assembly, is composed of two houses. The upper house, or senate, has 36 members; 151 members sit in the lower house, or house of representatives. All members of the General Assembly are elected to two-year terms.

The state supreme court is the highest court in Connecticut's judicial system. Its six justices are nominated by the governor and approved by the legislature to serve terms of eight years. The superior court is the state's only general trial court. Connecticut also has several probate courts and municipal courts.

Elected officials in the executive branch of the government include the secretary of state, secretary of the treasury, comptroller, attorney general, and lieutenant governor. The governor, or chief executive, is elected to a four-year term and may serve two terms consecutively. With the approval of the legislature, the governor appoints most other important state officials. The governor may veto bills approved by the General

Connecticut's magnificent new Legislative Office Building, designed by the firm of Russell Gibson von Dohlen, is linked, both visually and physically, to the capitol. An underground concourse with a moving walkway connects the building to the capitol, and the golden capitol dome is always visible through the curved glass walls of the atrium.

Assembly, but this veto can be overturned by a two-thirds vote in both the senate and the house of representatives.

Connecticut has 8 counties and 169 towns. Many communities still operate under the town meeting form of government established by the original colonists. At town meetings, all adult citizens are free to discuss local issues and vote for officials, or selectmen, to carry out their wishes. There is no county government in Connecticut.

About one-third of Connecticut's revenue comes from federal grants and programs. The remainder is raised through taxes. Connecticut's sales tax is among the highest in the country. The state also levies high corporate income taxes and property taxes, and sponsors a weekly lottery. Connecticut is one of the few states that has no personal income tax.

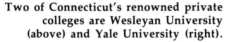

Two of Connecticut's renowned private colleges are Wesleyan University (above) and Yale University (right).

EDUCATION

The first school in Connecticut was founded in 1637. Today, all Connecticut children from the ages of seven through fifteen must attend school. In addition to its public school system, Connecticut has many nationally famous private academies, including the Choate School, in Wallingford; Kent Academy, in Kent; and Miss Porter's School for Girls, in Farmington. The American School for the Deaf, in West Hartford, was originally established in Hartford in 1817 as the country's first free school for deaf children.

Connecticut maintains state colleges in Danbury, New Haven, New Britain, and Willimantic. The University of Connecticut at Storrs began as an agricultural college, but expanded to offer a full

Cadets on parade at the United States
Coast Guard Academy in New London, one
of the nation's four service academies

liberal-arts curriculum. The Coast Guard Academy, at New
London, is one of four national military colleges.

Among Connecticut's private colleges are Trinity College, in
Hartford; Wesleyan University, in Middletown; and Yale
University, in New Haven. Yale's first classes were held at
present-day Clinton in 1701. The school moved to New Haven in
1716. Today, Yale is one of the world's most respected institutions
of higher learning. The university's many colleges include schools
of art, architecture, drama, music, nursing, medicine, law, and
business management. With more than eight million volumes,
Yale's Sterling Memorial Library has one of the largest collections
of books in the world. The remarkable Beinecke Rare Book and
Manuscript Library is a paradise for scholars and researchers.

Thousands of Connecticut commuters travel by rail to their jobs in New York.

TRANSPORTATION

Connecticut has about 19,000 miles (30,577 kilometers) of paved roads and highways. One of the main arteries of traffic is the Connecticut Turnpike (I-95 to Route 52), which spans the state from Greenwich, near the New York border, to Killingly, on the Rhode Island border. Other major highways are I-84, which crosses the state from Danbury to Union, and I-91, which runs north from the Connecticut Turnpike in New Haven all the way to the Vermont-Canada border. Passenger trains serve about forty-five towns and cities, and thousands of Connecticut commuters travel by rail to their jobs in New York.

Connecticut has 110 public and private airports. The largest is Bradley International Airport, in Windsor Locks near Hartford. Bridgeport, New Haven, and New London are major seaports. Small oceangoing ships can navigate the Connecticut River all the way to Hartford, 50 miles (80 kilometers) from the coast.

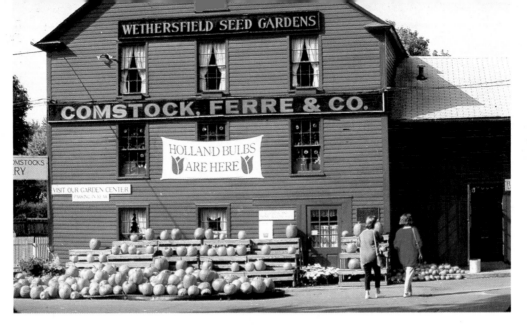

Pumpkins and other Connecticut farm products are sold throughout the state.

COMMUNICATION

The first issue of the *Connecticut Courant* appeared in 1764. The *Hartford Courant*, as it was later renamed, is the oldest continuously published newspaper in the United States. Other important papers in the state include the *Bridgeport Post*, the *New Haven Register*, and the *Waterbury Republican and American*.

Connecticut's first radio station, WDRC, went on the air in Hartford in 1922. Television came to the state in 1948 when WNHC-TV (now WTNH-TV) began broadcasting in New Haven. Today, Connecticut has about eighty radio stations and nine television stations.

AGRICULTURE

In Hartford's Old State House Square, vendors sell fresh corn, cucumbers, apples, and spinach from nearby farms in the Connecticut Valley. During the summer months, similar farmers' markets flourish throughout the state. Connecticut has some of the most valuable farmland in the United States, selling at $2,231 per acre (about $892 per hectare) in 1980. By comparison, farmland in Wyoming cost only $165 per acre (about $66 per hectare).

Nevertheless, agriculture accounts for less than one-half of 1 percent of Connecticut's gross state product (GSP), the total value of goods and services produced within the state during a given year. Connecticut's 3,800 farms are relatively small, averaging only 118 acres (48 hectares). Eggs are the state's most valuable farm product. Connecticut also has many dairy farms. The state is a leader in the production of shade-grown tobacco, which is used to make the outer wrappings of cigars. Apples, potatoes, sweet corn, and nursery products such as shrubs and flowers are other important sources of income.

MANUFACTURING

Manufacturing in Connecticut earns about $16.3 billion a year, 28 percent of the GSP. Factories employ about 26 percent of the state's labor force. Connecticut builds helicopters, jet engines, and submarines, largely under contract from the Department of Defense. The world's first atomic submarine, the USS *Nautilus*, was constructed at Groton and launched in 1954.

Connecticut leads the nation in the production of ball bearings. Nonelectrical machines manufactured in the state include planers, grinders, and lathes. Connecticut factories also assemble electrical conductors, outlets, and switches.

New Haven and New Britain are Connecticut's hardware centers, producing nuts, bolts, rivets, washers, and pipe fittings. Other manufactured products include processed foods, printed materials, and toys.

The Travelers Insurance Company Tower rises above the Hartford skyline.

SERVICE INDUSTRIES

Instead of manufacturing goods to be sold, service industries produce services for groups of individuals. In Connecticut, service industries account for 67 percent of the gross state product.

Connecticut's insurance business dates back to colonial times, when companies sold policies to insure clients against losses from fire. Today, Hartford is sometimes called the Insurance Capital of the World. More than fifty insurance companies are based in Hartford and its suburbs, including such giants as The Hartford, Travelers, and Aetna. Insurance, banking, and real estate make up about 21 percent of Connecticut's GSP, a larger percentage than in any other state except New York.

Wholesale and retail trade comprise the state's second most-valuable service industry. New Haven is a major center for the trade of fuel, lumber, and farm products. Other service industries include advertising, health care, education, and tourism.

77

Chapter 8
ARTS AND ENTERTAINMENT

ARTS AND ENTERTAINMENT

Small though it is, Connecticut has produced some of the nation's most outstanding figures in literature and the fine arts. Other writers and painters, born outside the state, have done some of their best work in Connecticut. In the performing arts, and in athletics as well, Connecticut has made significant contributions to American life.

LITERATURE

Life in Puritan Connecticut revolved around the church, and the colony's earliest literary efforts consisted of religious essays by such leaders as Thomas Hooker and John Davenport. By the 1700s, more earthly matters were addressed in the form of almanacs for farmers. The first of these, written by Daniel Travis in 1709, contains useful information about weather conditions, crop prices, and the distance between taverns along the colony's rutted roads.

During the 1730s and 1740s, Congregational pastor Jonathan Edwards, who was born in East Windsor, fired up the religious zeal of many New Englanders. In "Sinners in the Hands of an Angry God," a sermon that he delivered at Enfield in 1741, he terrified his listeners with the threat of eternal damnation: "The God that holds you over the pit of hell, much as one holds a spider or some loathsome insect over the fire, abhors you, and is dreadfully provoked." Edwards's preachings led to a religious revival known as the Great Awakening. He spent his last years as a missionary among the Indians in Stockbridge, Massachusetts. During that period of his life, he wrote his most famous religious treatise, "On Notions of Free Will."

Hartford became an important literary center in the years after the Revolutionary War. A group of intellectuals, often referred to as the Hartford Wits, met regularly at the Bunch of Grapes Tavern to discuss their works in progress. Among the group's prominent members was John Trumbull, nephew of Governor Jonathan Trumbull. John Trumbull's "The Progress of Dullness" is a lively satire about Yale University. Joel Barlow's epic about the conquest of North America, "The Columbiad," seems pretentious by modern standards. Barlow is more fondly remembered for "The Hasty Pudding," a humorous poem about eating corn pudding with a spoon. Another Hartford Wit was Dr. Lemuel Hopkins, an innovator in the treatment of tuberculosis, who attacked the charlatans in his profession with a satirical epitaph:

Here lies a fool flat on his back,
The victim of a cancer quack,
Who lost his money and his life
By plaster, caustic, and by knife.

Born in West Hartford, Noah Webster helped to validate and standardize American English. As a teacher, he wrote the *Blue-Backed Speller,* which some schools used well into the twentieth century. After twenty-five years of work, he published his massive *American Dictionary of the English Language* in 1828. The book included five thousand uniquely American words that had never appeared in any dictionary before. Webster's dictionary has been enlarged and revised countless times and is still an essential reference tool today.

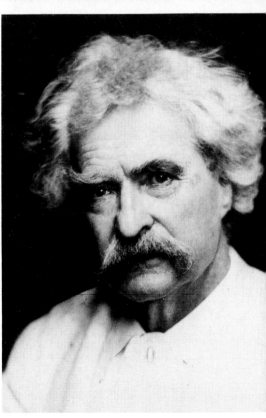

Connecticut writers who have made an impact on the nation over the years include (clockwise from top left) abolitionist Harriet Beecher Stowe; dictionary pioneer Noah Webster; novelist and humorist Samuel Clemens (Mark Twain); fiery Congregational pastor Jonathan Edwards; and Pulitzer Prizewinning poet Wallace Stevens.

Mark Twain's elaborate Victorian mansion at Nook Farm, in Hartford

Harriet Beecher Stowe, the daughter of a distinguished Congregational minister, grew up in Litchfield. In 1833, she moved to Cincinnati, Ohio, where she became involved in the antislavery movement. Her novel *Uncle Tom's Cabin*, which she wrote in 1851 in Maine, was a powerful indictment of slavery in southern society. The book, and the popular stage version of the story, heightened antislavery feelings in the North and is sometimes regarded as a precipitating cause of the Civil War. Stowe eventually returned to Connecticut and spent her last years in a writers' colony at Nook Farm, in Hartford.

Another prominent resident of Nook Farm was Samuel Clemens, who wrote his many novels and humorous sketches under the pen name Mark Twain. Mark Twain moved to Hartford in 1870 and settled at Nook Farm four years later. During his thirty years in Connecticut, he wrote some of his best-loved novels, including *The Adventures of Tom Sawyer* and *Adventures of Huckleberry Finn*. His *Connecticut Yankee in King Arthur's Court* is a tale of time travel in which a practical New Englander is swept back to the age of chivalry. Most critics consider Mark Twain to be one of America's greatest writers.

One of the greatest playwrights of the twentieth century was Eugene O'Neill. O'Neill spent his childhood traveling from town to town with his actor father. The only secure home he knew in his early years was the family's summer cottage in New London. Many of O'Neill's works, such as *The Iceman Cometh* and *Long Day's Journey into Night*, are grimly realistic dramas about human failure and despair. His only full-length comedy, *Ah, Wilderness!*, is set in New London and reveals his affectionate memories of the summers he spent there. O'Neill was the first serious dramatist in the American theater. During his career, he won the Pulitzer Prize in drama four times, and he was awarded the Nobel Prize in literature in 1936.

Wallace Stevens was a highly successful businessman who spent almost forty years working for a prominent Hartford insurance company. He was also one of the leading American poets of the twentieth century. He received the 1954 Pulitzer Prize in poetry for his *Collected Poems*. Stevens's poetry is highly intellectual and sometimes difficult to understand. It is chiefly concerned with the complex relationship between reality and the human imagination. In "An Ordinary Evening in New Haven," he writes:

> We keep coming back and coming back
> To the real: to the hotel instead of the hymns
> That fall upon it out of the wind.

Peter de Vries, a longtime resident of Westport, has been called by one critic the "greatest living American comic writer." In

Artist John Trumbull's best known painting is *The Signing of the Declaration of Independence,* which is based on portraits of the signers.

novels such as *Comfort Me with Apples, Through the Fields of Clover,* and *Forever Panting,* de Vries gently satirizes modern suburban life. Many of his works capture the atmosphere of the "bedroom communities" of Fairfield County.

ART

The names of Connecticut's first artists were not recorded for history. Some created small murals on the interior walls of colonial houses. Others traveled from farm to farm with bundles of canvas, painting family portraits.

The first Connecticut painter to achieve national recognition was John Trumbull of Lebanon, son of Governor Jonathan Trumbull and a cousin of poet John Trumbull. Trumbull the artist is best known for his painting *The Signing of the Declaration of Independence.* In 1817, Congress commissioned Trumbull to paint four scenes from the Revolutionary War for the rotunda of the Capitol in Washington, D.C.

Many of George Henry Durrie's winter landscapes became subjects of popular Currier and Ives prints.

John Frederick Kensett of Cheshire is one of the foremost nineteenth-century American landscape painters. Kensett's work is especially noted for its representation of light through the subtle use of color. Kensett captured scenes of the Great Lakes and New York's Catskill Mountains, but he rarely painted in his home state.

George Henry Durrie, on the other hand, drew the inspiration for his finest landscapes from the Connecticut countryside. Many of his winter scenes are familiar to Americans today as subjects of popular Currier and Ives prints.

During the 1890s, the charm of Connecticut's hills and seacoast began to attract American painters. Artists' colonies developed in Mystic, Old Lyme, Norwalk, and Cos Cob (now part of Greenwich). Artists are still drawn to these communities today. In many coastal towns, their work is exhibited at summer street festivals and in galleries throughout the year.

In 1910, Gutzon Borglum, the great sculptor, moved from New York to Stamford and built a studio. About one million visitors each year flock to the Black Hills of South Dakota to see his

Sculptor Gutzon Borglum created the Mount Rushmore National Memorial by carving the likenesses of Presidents George Washington, Thomas Jefferson, Theodore Roosevelt, and Abraham Lincoln into a granite cliff.

greatest work. Borglum designed the massive sculptures of the Mount Rushmore National Memorial, where the faces of four American presidents, each some 60 feet (18 meters) high, are carved into a granite cliff. The work was begun in 1927 and was not completed until 1941. Some of his other works can be seen today at the New Britain Museum of American Art.

PERFORMING ARTS

Music, dance, and theater flourish in Connecticut's cities. Hartford's Bushnell Memorial Auditorium hosts concerts by the Hartford Symphony Orchestra and performances by the Hartford Ballet. The Hartford Stage Company has its own theater in downtown Hartford. Bridgeport is home to the Greater Bridgeport Symphony and the Greater Bridgeport Ballet.

Yale University brings a wealth of cultural entertainment to New Haven throughout the year. Concerts on the campus range from eighteenth-century chamber music to atonal modern

The Yale Repertory Theatre, in New Haven

compositions. The Yale Repertory Theatre has been the first to perform works by some of the world's leading playwrights.

The New Haven Symphony is the fourth-oldest orchestra in the country. New Haven is also the home of the Orchestra of New England. The Long Wharf Theatre premieres many musicals, which later move on to Broadway.

Connecticut has many summer theater festivals. The American Festival Theater of Stratford performs Shakespearean dramas in an octagonal playhouse modeled on Shakespeare's Globe Theater at Stratford-on-Avon, in England. The Goodspeed Opera House in East Haddam is famous for its summer musical productions such as *Man of La Mancha* and *Annie*, both of which went on to open on Broadway.

SPORTS

The annual Harvard-Yale game is a college football tradition that dates back to 1875. The game no longer commands the attention of national sports fans because neither school is a

The annual Harvard-Yale football game is a tradition that dates back to 1875.

football powerhouse. Both schools are devoted to turning out
scholars instead of athletes. The first college football game at Yale
took place in 1872. In 1876, Yale, along with Harvard, Princeton,
and Columbia, organized the American Intercollegiate Football
Association, the nation's first college football conference. One Yale
football star, who played more than a hundred years ago, was
Walter Camp. In 1889, Camp and a sportswriter friend named the
nation's eleven best players at their various positions, and thereby
started the tradition of picking the All-American Football Team.

In modern times, Yale, the University of Connecticut, and
Wesleyan all have programs in football, basketball, baseball, and
other competitive sports. The University of Connecticut Huskies
have fielded powerful teams in the past, but have never won a
national championship in football.

Connecticut's only professional sports team is the Hartford
Whalers of the National Hockey League. The great Gordie Howe,
a hockey legend, ended his playing days with the Whalers. Pro
basketball fans in the state cheer for the Boston Celtics. Each
season the Celtics play several games at Hartford's Civic Center.

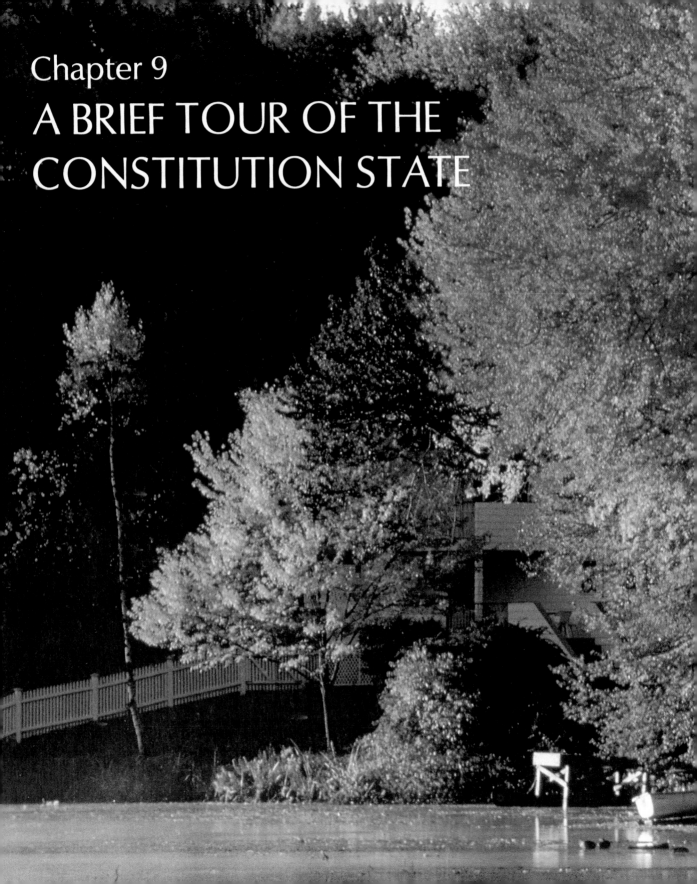

Chapter 9
A BRIEF TOUR OF THE CONSTITUTION STATE

A BRIEF TOUR OF THE CONSTITUTION STATE

From the Taconic Mountains to the rocky Thimble Islands, Connecticut is a state of rare natural beauty. Its long and fascinating history comes to life in countless museums and historic buildings. With its tiny villages that seem forgotten by time, its glass and steel skyscrapers, and its shining beaches, Connecticut has something to appeal to every taste.

THE CONNECTICUT COAST

In the southeastern corner of Connecticut, not far from the Rhode Island border, lies the town of Mystic. The town's historic district, Mystic Seaport, re-creates a nineteenth-century whaling village, complete with shops, horse-drawn carriages, and Victorian homes. Some three hundred vessels ride at anchor in Mystic Harbor, including fishing schooners, a coal-fired steamship, and the *Charles W. Morgan*, the world's only surviving wooden whaler.

The twin cities of Groton and New London face each other across the mouth of the Thames River. The world's first atomic submarine, the USS *Nautilus*, was launched from Groton in 1954. At the USS *Nautilus* Memorial, visitors can explore an authentic submarine control room and peer through a periscope at the underwater landscape. New London is the home of the United States Coast Guard Academy, which offers daily tours and a film

Mystic Seaport attractions include the wooden whaling ship *Charles W. Morgan*, carriage rides, and antique figureheads.

about cadet life. Another point of interest in New London is Monte Cristo, the boyhood home of playwright Eugene O'Neill.

Old Lyme, at the mouth of the Connecticut River, was the site of the state's first artists' colony. This picturesque village by the sea continues to attract painters and sculptors today. The Lyme

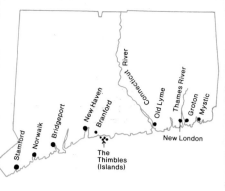

An outdoor art class
at the Lyme Academy of
Fine Arts, in Old Lyme

Academy of Fine Arts and the Florence Griswold Museum exhibit work by little-known local artists and by others who are already widely recognized.

The Harrison House, in Branford, is typical of the colonial saltbox houses that have survived throughout Connecticut. It is a square, stone dwelling built around a massive central chimney. Like dozens of other early homes in the state, Harrison House has been painstakingly restored.

Local people claim there are 365 Thimble Islands, one for each day of the year, clustered off the coast near Branford. The Thimbles are outcroppings of granite thrusting up from the ocean floor. The largest has an area of only 18 acres (7 hectares). According to legend, pirate Captain Kidd buried his treasure on one of the islands, but no one has ever found it.

Surveyed in 1640, New Haven is America's oldest planned city. The Green, or central square, is the heart of the city today. In the middle of the New Haven Green stands the Center Church, adorned with a large stained-glass window commemorating John Davenport and New Haven's first Puritan settlers.

One could spend a lifetime exploring the extraordinary libraries and museums at New Haven's Yale University. The Sterling Memorial Library houses the sixth-largest collection of books in

The New Haven Green, with its three historic churches, marks the center of the city.

the world. Among the treasures at the Beinecke Rare Book and Manuscript Library are a Gutenberg Bible from the fifteenth century, a portfolio of Audubon's original paintings of American birds, and a collection of Eugene O'Neill's letters and manuscripts. The Yale University Art Gallery is the nation's oldest college art museum. Founded in 1832 with a collection of paintings donated by John Trumbull, the museum displays early and modern works from every region of the globe. The Yale Center for British Art, which opened in 1972, houses a unique collection of work by English masters from the Elizabethan Age to the mid-nineteenth century. Exhibits at Yale's Peabody Museum of Natural History include dioramas of desert, forest, and mountain habitats, and the fossilized remains of a 6,000-pound (2,722-kilogram) ancient turtle.

Bridgeport is the largest and most heavily industrialized city in Connecticut. It is sometimes called Park City, because nearly

The P. T. Barnum Museum, in downtown Bridgeport, contains circus memorabilia.

2,000 acres (809 hectares) of land are set aside for municipal parks. Seaside Park is a 2-mile (3-kilometer) strip of beach donated by Bridgeport's most famous resident, circus manager P. T. Barnum. The P. T. Barnum Museum in downtown Bridgeport contains memorabilia from Barnum's show, including diminutive clothes worn by General Tom Thumb. Barnum's Tom Thumb was actually Charles Stratton, a Bridgeport native, who stood only 28 inches (71 centimeters) tall when he was fully grown.

An entire block of eighteenth-century buildings stands intact in Norwalk's historic district. The town's seafaring days are recalled in the Maritime History Center on the waterfront, where skilled artisans demonstrate boat-building techniques. The Lockwood-Mathews Mansion Museum preserves the fifty-room dream palace of a nineteenth-century financier, built around a vast rotunda with a 42-foot (13-meter) skylit ceiling.

Fine examples of colonial quilts, costumes, and dolls are displayed at the Stamford Historical Society. Stamford's First Presbyterian Church, dedicated in 1958, is sometimes called the

A carousel horse at
the United House
Wrecking Company,
a huge flea market
in Stamford

Fish Church because of its unusual shape. Embedded in the
church wall are one hundred stone tablets, each depicting a leader
in the Judeo-Christian heritage. The visitor to Stamford who has
grown weary of history and culture can browse for hours at the
United House Wrecking Company, a sprawling flea market that
overflows with antiques, toys, musical instruments, kitchenware,
and almost everything else imaginable.

THE WESTERN UPLAND

Western Connecticut is scored by narrow river valleys and
rugged hills. In the years before the Revolutionary War,

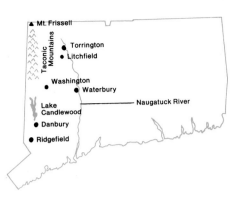

A British cannonball remains embedded in the cornerpost of the Keeler Tavern in Ridgefield.

Connecticut patriots often gathered at the Keeler Tavern in Ridgefield, not far from the New York border. British troops fired on the tavern in 1777, and a cannonball is still embedded in the cornerpost. With its taproom, ladies' parlor, and ample kitchen, the inn has been fully restored.

The city of Danbury, at the southern tip of Lake Candlewood, was once the hat-making capital of America. The Scott-Fanton Museum and Historical Society includes the complete restoration of a hat shop dating to 1790. The museum also contains memorabilia of American composer Charles Ives, a Danbury native who won the 1947 Pulitzer Prize in music.

One of Connecticut's most unusual museums is the American Indian Archaeological Institute, in Washington on the Shepaug River. In addition to a reconstructed Indian village, the institute demonstrates archaeological methods through a simulated dig at an ancient campsite. The institute also serves as a research center and conducts many educational programs about Indian cultures.

Above: The Tapping Reeve House (right) and Law School (left), in Litchfield, the site of the first school of law in the country

Left: The American Clock and Watch Museum, in Bristol, displays a variety of timepieces, from pocket watches to grandfather clocks.

Waterbury, on the Naugatuck River, was once the center of America's brass industry. The Mattatuck Museum reflects Waterbury's long history as the Brass City and displays the work of many Connecticut artists. Connecticut's prominence in clock manufacturing is evident at the American Clock and Watch Museum in Bristol. The museum displays nearly eighteen hundred timepieces, from pocket watches to stately grandfather clocks. Many were fashioned by such outstanding Connecticut clock makers as Eli Terry.

Some 4,000 acres (1,619 hectares) of woods and streams near Litchfield are preserved by the White Memorial Foundation as the largest nature center in Connecticut. Litchfield was the site of the Tapping Reeve Law School, the first school of law in America, which opened in 1774. The Tapping Reeve House and Law School are open to the public, and visitors can see the downstairs parlor where such distinguished graduates as Aaron Burr and John C. Calhoun once studied.

Picture-book country towns lie tucked among the green hills of northwestern Connecticut. West of Torrington spreads the Mohawk State Forest, where miles of hiking trails wind among stands of hardwoods, along bubbling streams and past half-hidden ponds. To the north, where the Taconic Mountains spill across the New York border, stands Mount Frissell, the highest point in Connecticut.

THE CENTRAL VALLEY

The Central Valley was carved over thousands of years by the slow, steady action of the Connecticut River. The rich, fertile land of the valley is highly valuable for farming. The Central Valley was the site of some of Connecticut's earliest European settlements and is one of the most densely populated regions of the state today.

A few miles south of the Massachusetts border, the Connecticut River foams into rapids near the town of Enfield. Below the rapids, the river becomes broad and smooth. The town of Warehouse Point is home to two unusual museums. The Warehouse Point Trolley Museum traces the history of the trolley from 1884 to 1947 and offers rides on some of its authentic trolley cars. The Connecticut Fire Museum documents the history of firefighting in the state, and houses a collection of fire engines dating back to 1850.

In 1775, the Connecticut patriots converted an old copper mine near East Granby into a prison for Tories and captured British soldiers. By day, the prisoners were forced to mine copper, and by

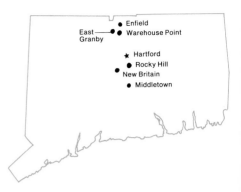

The predawn skyline of
Hartford, the capital

night they were chained to the walls in damp, icy tunnels. Today,
visitors to the Old New-Gate Prison and Copper Mine can
descend 200 feet (61 meters) into the gloomy labyrinth where the
prisoners lived, and shudder at the rusting chains still fastened to
the clammy walls.

Hartford, the state capital, is the hub of business and trade in
Connecticut. More insurance companies operate in Hartford than
in any other city in the world. The gilded dome of the state
capitol, completed in 1879, soars above the green oblong of
Bushnell Park. The Hall of Flags in the capitol displays the flags
that Connecticut troops carried into battle in each of the nation's
wars.

The governor's chair in the state capitol is made from the wood
of the great hollow oak tree that once hid Connecticut's precious
Royal Charter of 1662. The tree blew down in a storm in 1856, but
a tablet on Charter Oak Avenue marks the spot where it stood.
Humorist Mark Twain once remarked that he had seen enough
walking sticks, dog collars, three-legged stools, dinner tables, and

A carving of the Charter Oak appears on the capitol building in Hartford.

toothpicks supposedly made from the Charter Oak "to build a plank road from Hartford to Salt Lake City."

The original 1662 Royal Charter, the Fundamental Orders of 1639, and many other historic documents are housed at the Connecticut State Library. Nine galleries in the Museum of Connecticut History, located in the Connecticut State Library, display early coins, firearms, clocks, furniture, and the portraits of most of Connecticut's governors. The Connecticut Historical Society presents changing exhibits related to the history of the state and a permanent display of seventeenth- and eighteenth-century Connecticut furniture.

Founded in 1842, Hartford's Wadsworth Atheneum is the oldest free public art museum in the nation. The Atheneum houses a priceless collection of more than forty thousand works, from ancient Egyptian statues to abstract modern paintings and intricate collages.

Hartford's literary heritage is kept alive at Nook Farm, where some of America's most prominent writers lived in the late

The Wadsworth Atheneum is the nation's oldest free public art museum.

nineteenth century. Harriet Beecher Stowe's large, but simple, home contains much of its original furniture, as well as a collection of her papers and other belongings. In contrast, the house where Mark Twain wrote *The Adventures of Huckleberry Finn* is a lavish mansion with turrets and balconies. Other members of the Nook Farm community included novelist and editor Charles Dudley Warner and playwright William Gillette.

Noah Webster, who compiled the first dictionary of American English, was a resident of West Hartford. His home is a typical colonial farmhouse built around a central chimney. Volunteers at the house run workshops on basket making, spinning, and other early American crafts. Visitors may try carding wool by hand or taste a piping-hot hoecake cooked over the kitchen fire.

Visitors can read chapters from Connecticut's ancient past at Dinosaur State Park near Rocky Hill, just south of Hartford. The giant tracks of dinosaurs, which walked 185 million years ago, are protected under plexiglass domes. Visitors are invited to make plaster casts of some of these immense footprints.

Just west of Rocky Hill, New Britain celebrates man's conquest of space at the Copernican Space Science Center, which boasts the second-largest public telescope in the United States. The museum also has an excellent planetarium. The New Britain Museum of American Art displays more than five thousand works by the nation's masters, including John Singleton Copley, Gilbert Stuart, Gutzon Borglum, and Andrew Wyeth.

Farther south on the Connecticut River, Wesleyan University brings a wealth of concerts and plays to the city of Middletown. Wesleyan's Davison Art Center includes galleries of contemporary paintings, prints, and photographs. Connecticut's role in the development of the submarine is documented at the Submarine Library Museum, which maintains extensive files on American and foreign submarines.

THE EASTERN UPLAND

At Middletown, the Connecticut River leaves the Central Valley and veers into the wooded hills of the Eastern Upland. Legends abound along the Connecticut's southern reaches, where the river twists through a maze of inlets and wooded islands. In colonial times, many people believed that witchcraft flourished in and around Haddam. According to one story, the devil sometimes sat at the top of Chapman Falls, playing his violin while the witches prepared magic brews under the full moon. Devil's Hopyard State Park in East Haddam is named for this eerie tale.

These stories of witchcraft may have been inspired by the frightening underground rumblings occasionally heard around Haddam and Moodus, a neighboring town to the northeast. The explanation for these weird noises is probably geological rather than supernatural, as the region lies along a fault line in the

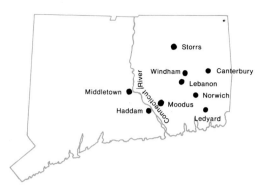

Devil's Hopyard State Park, in East Haddam

earth's crust. In 1791, a series of violent earth tremors near Moodus opened crevices in the ground, shattered windows, and toppled chimneys.

Ledyard, in the state's southeastern corner, offers a glimpse of colonial life at its Sawmill Park. The park contains a restored water-powered sawmill where raw logs are shaped into boards. At the park's blacksmith shop, molten iron is shaped into horseshoes.

The Indian Burial Grounds in Norwich, north of Ledyard, is the final resting place of Uncas, the Mohegan chief who aided the Puritan settlers in their war against the Pequots. Norwich's Leffingwell Inn served as a meeting place for the Sons of Liberty in the years after the Stamp Act was passed.

During the Revolutionary War, Governor Jonathan Trumbull's home in Lebanon was the scene of many meetings of such leading patriots as John Adams, Benjamin Franklin, and George Washington. Today, Jonathan Trumbull's house looks very much as it did in 1776, with many original furnishings from the Trumbull family. Nearby stands the War Office—Jonathan Trumbull's shipping business office—which was used as the headquarters for Connecticut's Council of Safety during the American Revolution.

Northeast of Lebanon lies the town of Windham. Late one night during the French and Indian War (1756-63), the people of Windham awoke to a din of roaring and moaning that came from the surrounding woods. Convinced that the sounds were Indian war whoops, the townspeople grabbed their guns and rushed into the streets. The noise lasted all night long, but no Indians appeared. When the sun rose, the townspeople searched the woods for the source of the commotion. On the banks of a nearby pond and floating on the water they discovered hundreds of bullfrogs, all of them dead. To this day, scientists do not know why the frogs made so much noise that night, or what caused them all to die. But the story lives on in Windham. A bullfrog is engraved on the town's official seal, and a plaque at the frog pond commemorates that long-ago night of needless terror.

Displays at the Prudence Crandall House in Canterbury, due east of Windham, recall the story of the courageous teacher who tried in vain to establish a school for black girls in 1833. About 17 miles (27 kilometers) to the northwest, the story of another Connecticut hero comes to life at the Nathan Hale Homestead in Coventry. The house was built in 1776 by Nathan Hale's father and contains many original furnishings and documents.

North of Coventry is Storrs, a lively college town and home of the main campus of the University of Connecticut. The university offers a fascinating array of concerts, films, plays, and lectures.

A stone wall in the woods near New Preston

Storrs is also known for the Connecticut State Museum of Natural History. The museum's extensive collections include minerals, fossils, Indian artifacts, mounted birds, and a great white shark killed off the Rhode Island-Connecticut coast.

In Connecticut's eastern section are the Natchaug and Pachaug state forests, where hikers can hear the calls of birds, the gurgle of streams, and the sigh of the wind in the branches overhead. Wandering these wooded hills, one can try to imagine how all of Connecticut looked in the 1630s, when the first European settlers arrived and began to clear the forests that seemed to stretch on forever.

Connecticut is one of the smallest states in the nation, but it makes no apologies for its size. The Constitution State has given the country inventors, patriots, writers, and scholars. In business and education, it is a national leader. With pride in their heritage, the people of Connecticut face the challenges of the years ahead.

FACTS AT A GLANCE

GENERAL INFORMATION

Statehood: January 9, 1788, fifth state

Origin of Name: From an Indian word, *Quinnehtukgut,* meaning "beside the long tidal river"

State Capital: Hartford, since 1875. From 1701 to 1875, Hartford and New Haven were twin capitals.

State Nickname: "Constitution State," from having the first written constitution in the New World and for working out the Connecticut Compromise, or Great Compromise, at the Constitutional Convention

State Flag: The state flag contains a white shield bordered with gold trim and green grape leaves inside a blue field. Three grapevines, representing the European culture that was transplanted to the colony of Connecticut, are inside the shield. Below the shield lies a banner with the state motto. The flag was adopted in 1897.

State Motto: *Qui Transtulit Sustinet* (He who transplanted still sustains)

State Bird: American robin

State Flower: Mountain laurel

State Tree: White oak

State Animal: Sperm whale

State Insect: Praying mantis

State Mineral: Garnet

State Ship: USS *Nautilus*

State Hero: Nathan Hale

State Song: "Yankee Doodle," composer unknown, adopted as state song in 1978:

> Yankee Doodle went to town
> Riding on a pony,
> Stuck a feather in his cap
> And called it macaroni.
>
> Yankee Doodle, keep it up,
> Yankee Doodle dandy,
> Mind the music and the step,
> And with the girls be handy.

POPULATION

Population: 3,107,576, twenty-fifth among the states (1980 census)

Population Density: 619 persons per sq. mi. (239 per km²)

Population Distribution: Tiny Connecticut is one of the most densely populated states in the nation. More than three of every four Connecticut residents (79 percent in 1980) live in cities or towns. Many of these residents are suburbanites who work in New York City. Bridgeport is the largest city.

Bridgeport	142,546
Hartford	136,392
New Haven	126,101
Waterbury	103,266
Stamford	102,466
Norwalk	77,767
New Britain	73,840
West Hartford	61,301
Danbury	60,470
Greenwich	59,578

(Population figures according to 1980 census)

Population Growth: Connecticut's population grew slowly but steadily from statehood until the late 1800s. Then immigrants from southern and eastern Europe streamed into the state, and the rate of growth increased. Another spurt of rapid growth took place after World War II. Many New York City families had automobiles and were able to afford homes in Connecticut, away from the more crowded city. Rapid growth continued through 1970, but the population has leveled off since then. The list on the next page shows the state's population growth since 1790:

Year	Population
1790	237,946
1800	251,002
1820	275,248
1840	309,978
1860	460,147
1880	622,700
1900	908,420
1920	1,380,631
1940	1,709,242
1950	2,007,280
1960	2,535,234
1970	3,032,217
1980	3,107,576

GEOGRAPHY

Borders: Connecticut is bordered by New York on the west, Massachusetts on the north, and Rhode Island on the east. Long Island Sound, a part of the Atlantic Ocean, borders Connecticut on the south.

Highest Point: Mount Frissell, 2,380 ft. (725 m) above sea level

Lowest Point: Sea level, at Long Island Sound

Greatest Distances: North to south—75 mi. (121 km)
East to west—90 mi. (145 km)

Area: 5,018 sq. mi. (12,997 km²)

Rank in Area Among the States: Forty-eighth

Rivers: Connecticut has about 8,400 mi. (13,518 km) of rivers and streams. The Connecticut, the longest river in New England, cuts through the heart of the state. Some oceangoing ships sail as far north as Hartford, 50 mi. (80 km) inland. The Thames and Quinebaug are major rivers of eastern Connecticut. The Housatonic and Naugatuck flow through western Connecticut.

Lakes: Connecticut has more than 1,000 lakes, most of them small bodies of glacial origin. Bantam Lake, near Litchfield, is the largest of these natural lakes. Artificially created Lake Candlewood, a reservoir used to store water for generating power, is the largest lake in the state. It measures 8 sq. mi. (21 km²).

A lighthouse on the Connecticut River estuary

Coasts: Connecticut has 618 mi. (994 km) of shoreline in the form of coast, offshore islands, sounds, and bays along Long Island Sound. Greenwich, Stamford, Norwalk, Bridgeport, New Haven, and New London have fine harbors along the coast.

Topography: Although tiny compared to other states, Connecticut has five land regions. The extreme northwest corner of the state contains the Taconic Section, part of the Taconic Mountains. Connecticut's highest elevation, Mt. Frissell, is found here.

Heavy forests and rugged, rocky hills mark the Western New England Upland. This region covers the western third of the state. The Housatonic, Naugatuck, and other rivers flow through the Western New England Upland.

The Connecticut Valley Lowland, or Central Valley, begins at New Haven and extends into Massachusetts. This central region has both level terrain and rolling hills. Soil varies from rich loam to sandy. Ridges that resisted the Connecticut River rise 300 to 600 ft. (91 to 183 m) above the river.

Eastern Connecticut is covered by the Eastern New England Upland. This region includes rolling land with narrow valleys and low hills.

A Coastal Plain borders Long Island Sound. The narrow band, only 6 to 16 mi. (10 to 26 km) wide, has lower and smoother land than the state's other regions. Low ridges, beaches, bays, and harbors appear along the coast.

Climate: Connecticut, although a small state, has some climatic variations. The northwestern part of the state, more mountainous and in the path of cold winds, may see extreme cold. The coast may see cooler summer temperatures because of the cool summer winds. The central portion of the state usually has the hottest summer temperatures. Hartford, near the center of the state, has average temperatures varying from 74° F. (23° C) in July to 27° F. (-3° C) in January. Bridgeport, along the coast, has temperatures ranging from 73° F. (23° C) in July to 30° F. (-1° C) in January. Connecticut averages about 46 in. (117 cm) of precipitation, including about 25 in. (64 cm) of snow, although the northwestern mountains may receive 80 in. (203 cm) of snow annually. The western highlands and Connecticut River valley are occasionally visited by tornadoes. Hurricanes may appear on the coast, and sometimes they intrude inland.

NATURE

Trees: Forests cover more than 60 percent of Connecticut. Trees include ash, beech, birch, elm, hemlock, hickory, maple, oak, pine, cedar, sycamore, basswood, hop hornbean, ironwood, willow, and horse chestnut.

Wild Plants: Mountain laurel, dogwood, bayberry, sheep laurel, sweet fern, wild cherry, huckleberry, blueberry, black raspberry, juniper berry, trailing arbutus, hepatica, cowslip, bloodroot, Indian pipe, lupine, jack-in-the-pulpit, pennyroyal, lady's slipper

Animals: Human beings have chased away many large species from Connecticut lands, but the state still has foxes, skunks, muskrats, woodchucks, raccoons, opossums, squirrels, cottontail rabbits, white-tailed deer, beavers, otters, and minks. Lobsters, oysters, and clams are plentiful in coastal waters.

Birds: Ducks, partridges, ring-necked pheasants, ruffed grouse, orioles, sparrows, thrushes, warblers, hawks, owls, woodpeckers, robins, bluebirds, bluejays, crows, meadowlarks, goldfinches, chickadees, quails, woodcocks, bobwhites, whippoorwills, cardinals

Fish: Among the many Connecticut freshwater fish are shad, largemouth and smallmouth bass, pickerel, perch, bullhead, calico bass, pike, sockeye salmon, bluegill, sunfish, and brook, brown, and rainbow trout. Saltwater fish include flounder, blackfish, striped bass, bluefish, smelt, mackerel, porgy, swordfish, butterfish, cod, and pollack.

GOVERNMENT

Connecticut has had four constitutions. The first, called the Fundamental Orders, was adopted in 1639. Some historians consider the Fundamental Orders to be the world's first written constitution. This set of laws served until 1662, when a royal charter became the ruling document. A third constitution, which extended voting rights, was adopted in 1818. The present constitution was approved by voters in 1965. It requires that voters decide every twenty years whether to call a constitutional convention.

Like the federal government, Connecticut's government is divided into three branches. The legislative (lawmaking) branch is called the General Assembly. This body has a 36-member senate and a 151-member house of representatives. All General Assembly members serve two-year terms.

The executive branch enforces the laws. The governor may veto laws, but that veto may be overridden by a two-thirds vote of both houses of the legislature. The governor, lieutenant governor, attorney general, comptroller, secretary of state, and state treasurer are elected to four-year terms and may be reelected.

Courts form the judicial branch. The supreme court and appellate court each have six judges. The superior court, which hears major criminal and civil cases, has 131 members. Judges on these courts are nominated by the governor and approved by the General Assembly to eight-year terms. Probate-court judges are elected by the voters and serve four-year terms.

Number of Counties: 8

U.S. Representatives: 6

Electoral Votes: 8

Voting Qualifications: Citizen of the United States, eighteen years of age, registered to vote twenty-one days before an election, registered with party enrollment one day before a primary election

EDUCATION

Connecticut is a state long renowned for its high quality of education. State law requires children to attend school from age seven through fifteen. About 375,000 students attend Connecticut elementary schools. Another 175,000 students are in secondary schools. About 88,000 of these students are in private schools. Connecticut students are taught by about 38,200 teachers. Each year, the state spends more than $3,500 per pupil on education.

A commissioner of education and a nine-member board of education supervise the public school system in Connecticut. The governor appoints the board members to a four-year term, and the board members elect the commissioner to the same term.

Connecticut has about twenty-five colleges and universities. World-famous Yale University, in New Haven, is the best known. Others include Albertus Magnus College and Southern Connecticut State University, in New Haven; the University of Bridgeport, Bridgeport Engineering Institute, and Sacred Heart University, in Bridgeport; Central Connecticut State University, in New Britain; Charter Oak College, Hartford Graduate Center, Hartford Seminary, and Trinity College, in Hartford; the University of Connecticut, in Storrs; Connecticut College and the United States Coast Guard Academy, in New London; Eastern Connecticut State University, in Willimantic; Fairfield University, in Fairfield; the University of

Hartford and St. Joseph College, in West Hartford; Holy Apostles College, in Cromwell; the University of New Haven, in West Haven; Post College, in Waterbury; Quinnipiac College, in Hamden; St. Alphonsus College, in Suffield; Wesleyan University, in Middletown; and Western Connecticut State University, in Danbury.

ECONOMY AND INDUSTRY

Principal Products:

Agriculture: Eggs and other poultry products, milk and other dairy products, tobacco, apples, potatoes, sweet corn, cattle, hogs, sheep, hay, berries, blueberries, feed corn, nursery products

Manufacturing: Helicopters, jet aircraft engines, propellers, submarines, grinders, lathes, planers, ball bearings, roller bearings, electrical conductors, outlets, switches, generators, household appliances, lighting fixtures, motors, bolts, nuts, rivets, washers, valve fittings, pipe fittings, processed copper, chemicals, food products, toys, printed materials

Mining: Stone, traprock, sand, gravel, feldspar, clay, gemstones, mica

Business and Trade: Manufacturing accounts for the largest portion of the Connecticut economy. Manufacturing produces about 28 percent of the gross state product (GSP) and employs about 26 percent of the work force. Bridgeport, Danbury, Groton, New London, Meriden, Hartford, New Britain, New Haven, Stamford, Stratford, and Waterbury are all manufacturing centers. Finance, insurance, and real estate account for about 21 percent of the GSP. These industries employ 8 percent of the state's work force. Another 16 percent of the GSP comes from wholesale and retail trade. These jobs employ 22 percent of Connecticut residents. Community, social, and personal services contribute 15 percent of the GSP and employ 22 percent of the work force. Government accounts for 8 percent of the GSP and employs 12 percent of the work force. Transportation, communication, and utilities produce about 7 percent of the GSP and employ 5 percent of the work force. Construction, mining, and agriculture contribute 5 percent of the GSP and employ 5 percent of the work force.

Hartford is the headquarters for about fifty insurance companies, including several of the largest in the nation. Fairfield County, because of its open space and nearness to New York City, is attracting many corporate headquarters.

Finance: Connecticut has about 15 national banks with 373 branches, 52 state banks with 316 branches, and 57 mutual savings banks with 441 branches. The Constitution State also has 35 savings and loan associations with 150 branches.

Communication: The *Connecticut Courant* (now *Hartford Courant*), established in 1764, is the oldest continuously published daily newspaper in the country. About eighty other newspapers, including about twenty-five dailies, now also serve Connecticut. Other newspapers include the *Bridgeport Post, New Haven Register,* and *Waterbury Republican and American.*

Connecticut residents have a choice of many radio and television stations. The state's residents also may tune into dozens of stations from New York or Boston.

Hartford's WDRC, established in 1922, is Connecticut's oldest radio station. WNHC (now WTNH-TV) of New Haven, started in 1948, is the oldest television station in the state.

Transportation: Connecticut serves as a transportation link between New England and New York City and the rest of the nation. The state has about 19,000 mi. (30,577 km) of roads and highways. Interstate 95 follows the coast from Greenwich to the Rhode Island border. Interstate 84 runs from Danbury to Union. Interstate 91 begins at New Haven and runs north to the Massachusetts border.

The first important Connecticut railroad, the Hartford and New Haven, began service in 1838. Trains now carry thousands of residents each day to their jobs in Connecticut or New York City. Passenger trains serve about forty-five Connecticut towns and cities. Four railroads provide freight service. About 110 public and private airports serve the state. Bradley International Airport in Windsor Locks provides air service between Connecticut and fifty U.S. cities.

Sea commerce is also important to Connecticut. Bridgeport, New Haven, and New London handle about 20 million tons (18 million metric tons) of cargo annually.

SOCIAL AND CULTURAL LIFE

Museums: Connecticut has a rich, varied culture and works hard to preserve that heritage in its many museums. The Connecticut Historical Society, with historical exhibits and an extensive research library, and the Old State House, both in Hartford, provide rich information on Connecticut history. The Museum of Connecticut History, at the Connecticut State Library in Hartford, contains documents, old coins and medals, historical artifacts, and Abraham Lincoln materials. The Henry Whitfield House, in Guilford, the oldest house in the state and perhaps the oldest stone house in the nation, is a state-owned historical property. Nathan Hale's home, in Coventry, honors the Revolutionary War patriot. Many other preserved homes depict life in early Connecticut days. The American Indian Archaeological Institute, in Washington, shows the civilization of Connecticut's first residents.

Hartford's Wadsworth Atheneum boasts of being America's oldest free art museum. Works of European and American masters are displayed in this renowned museum. Yale University, in New Haven, has a famous art gallery, as well as the Yale Center for British Art. Mattatuck Museum, in Waterbury, focuses on the work of Connecticut artists. Art museums also may be found in New Britain, New London, Stamford, Middletown, and Farmington.

The Peabody Museum, in New Haven, part of Yale University, contains one of the finest natural-history collections in the world. The Bruce Museum, in Greenwich, is another excellent natural-history museum.

Connecticut museums also cover other aspects of life. East Windsor and Warehouse Point boast fire museums. Visitors may view a farm-implement museum in Bloomfield. Warehouse Point, East Haven, and East Windsor have trolley museums. The American Clock and Watch Museum, in Bristol, owns a collection of clocks dating from the 1700s. Terryville's Lock Museum of America has the largest collection of locks, keys, and ornate hardware in the nation.

Hot-air ballooning in Norwalk

Libraries: Early Connecticut libraries were privately owned. The first public library was organized at Durham in 1733. Salisbury opened the Scoville Library in 1803. It was the first tax-supported library in the United States. Connecticut now has about two hundred public libraries plus branch libraries and bookmobiles for remote areas.

Yale University has the oldest library in the state. Its Sterling Memorial Library contains eight million volumes, making it one of the largest in the world. The Sterling Library and Yale's Beinecke Rare Book and Manuscript Collection both have famed collections of English books and manuscripts.

Trinity College Library, in Hartford, has many Episcopal church materials. The Connecticut State Library, also in Hartford, holds many historical materials, including the original copy of the Royal Charter of 1662. Hartford also has many law and insurance libraries.

Mystic Seaport Library specializes in maritime history. The Wilbur Cross Library at the University of Connecticut, in Storrs, houses an extensive collection of materials.

Performing Arts: The Goodspeed Opera Company runs summer plays in East Haddam. The Eugene O'Neill Theatre Foundation sponsors an active program in Waterford. The Long Wharf Theatre and Yale Repertory Theatre, in New Haven, and the Hartford Stage Company are other professional theaters. Connecticut College annually sponsors the American Dance Festival in New London.

Hartford, New Haven, New London, Norwalk, Stamford, and Waterbury all have symphony orchestras. Summer concerts are held at Music Mountain, in Canaan; the Silvermine Guild of Artists, in New Canaan; and the Norfolk Music Shed. Musicians also perform regularly at many clubs throughout the state.

Sports and Recreation: Hockey is a mania in Connecticut, and fans from the Constitution State flock to see the National Hockey League's Hartford Whalers. Hockey is also played at the minor-league, college, and high-school levels throughout the state. The National Basketball Association's Boston Celtics sometimes play "home" games in Hartford. Baseball and football fans cheer for professional teams from nearby Boston and New York. Yale University provides Ivy League college football, including its annual game with longtime rival Harvard.

Connecticut rivers provide excellent trout, salmon, and perch fishing. Anglers also may use boats from Niantic, Stonington, and Mystic for deep-sea fishing. Hunting, sailing, yachting, curling, golf, and jai alai are other popular sports.

Hikers, campers, swimmers, and nature lovers have many sites from which to enjoy the outdoors. Lighthouse Point Park, near New Haven, offers swimming, natural-history displays, and a turn-of-the-century beach pavilion with a carousel. Connecticut has about 120 state parks and recreation areas and 29 state forests. Devil's Hopyard State Park, near East Haddam, contains Chapman Falls and a spectacular gorge. Putnam Memorial State Park, in Bethel, is the site where General Israel Putnam and his troops endured the winter of 1777-78. Kent Falls State Park, in North Kent, has a waterfall that plunges more than a quarter of a mile (nearly half a kilometer).

Historic Sites and Landmarks:

Bush-Holley House, in Cos Cob, Greenwich, interprets the lives of three families during three centuries.

Groton Monument, in Groton, is a 134-foot (41-meter) granite tower that commemorates the 1781 Battle of Fort Griswold, where British troops under the command of traitorous General Benedict Arnold massacred captured American patriots.

Harriet Beecher Stowe House, at Nook Farm in Hartford, is the 1871 "cottage" that was the home of the author of *Uncle Tom's Cabin.*

Jonathan Trumbull House, in Lebanon, was a meeting place for leading patriots during the Revolutionary War.

Keeler Tavern, in Ridgefield, served as a popular eighteenth-century inn and meeting place.

Kent Furnace Site, at Kent, displays the ruins of an early iron furnace and a museum of early tools and implements.

Mark Twain House, at Nook Farm in Hartford, is the Victorian mansion that was the home of the famous American writer from 1874 to 1891.

Monte Cristo Cottage, in New London, was the boyhood residence of famed playwright Eugene O'Neill.

Mystic Seaport Museum, in Mystic, is a reconstruction of an 1800s whaling village.

Monte Cristo Cottage, the boyhood home of playwright Eugene O'Neill, was the setting for *Long Day's Journey Into Night*.

Noah Webster House and Museum, in West Hartford, is the eighteenth-century farmhouse that was the birthplace of the man who created America's first dictionary.

Ogden House, in Fairfield, is a well-preserved eighteenth-century saltbox farmhouse.

Old New-Gate Prison and Copper Mine, in East Granby, was the first American-chartered copper mine and later served as a Revolutionary War prison.

Old State House, in Hartford, the oldest state house in the nation, was the building used by Connecticut's early legislators.

Prudence Crandall House, in Canterbury, was the site of a short-lived academy for young black women.

Tapping Reeve House and Law School, in Litchfield, was the first law school in the United States.

Ye Olde Town Mill, in New London, built in 1650, depicts an early New England grist mill.

Twenty-four-room Gillette Castle, at Hadlyme, was built by nineteenth-century actor and playwright William Gillette.

Other Interesting Places to Visit:

Ancient Burying Ground, in Hartford, contains nearly four hundred distinctive gravestones displaying unique forms of American folk art.

Cattletown Movie Ranch, in Oneco, offers Wild West shows, gold panning, and buckboard rides.

Connecticut Arboretum, in New London, contains 425 acres (172 hectares) of trees, shrubs, hiking trails, and ponds.

Dinosaur State Park, at Rocky Hill, displays dinosaur footprints dating back 185 million years.

First Presbyterian Church, in Stamford, is a unique fish-shaped house of worship.

Gillette Castle State Park, at Hadlyme, has a twenty-four-room castle built by nineteenth-century actor and playwright William Gillette.

Housatonic Railroad Company, Union Station, in Canaan, is the oldest train station in continuous use (since 1872) in the United States.

Lock 12 Historical Park, in Cheshire, the restoration of a section of the nineteenth-century Farmington Canal, also contains a museum.

Mystic Marinelife Aquarium, in Mystic, shows more than five thousand specimens of living fish, sea mammals, and other marine life.

A circus wagon at the P. T. Barnum Museum, in Bridgeport

P. T. Barnum Museum, in Bridgeport, honors America's most famous showman.

Sawmill Park, in Ledyard, is an 11-acre (4-hectare) park with a restored colonial water-powered vertical saw and a blacksmith shop.

State Capitol, in Hartford, completed in 1879, has legislative chambers, executive offices, and items from the state's past.

United States Coast Guard Academy, in New London, is one of America's four military-service academies.

USS Nautilus Memorial, in Groton, has the world's first atomic submarine.

Yale University, in New Haven, considered one of the world's great universities, has a picturesque campus with world-famous libraries and art museums.

The first school in Connecticut was founded in 1637, and in 1650, a law was passed that required every town of fifty families or more to hire a teacher.

IMPORTANT DATES

1614 — Adriaen Block claims Connecticut for the Dutch

1633 — The English make the first settlement in Windsor; the Dutch establish a colony on the site of present-day Hartford

1636 — The towns of Hartford, Wethersfield, and Windsor unite to form the Connecticut Colony

1637 — Connecticut and other colonies join forces to defeat Indians in the Pequot War

1638 — Wealthy Puritans found a colony at Quinnipiac, the site of present-day New Haven; earthquake shakes southern Connecticut

1639 — Connecticut Colony adopts a constitution, the Fundamental Orders

1647 — Connecticut becomes the first New England colony to convict and hang a woman for practicing witchcraft

1650 — A law is passed that requires every town of fifty families or more to hire a teacher to instruct children in reading and writing

1654 — The English drive the Dutch from Connecticut

1657 — Shipbuilding begins at Derby

1662 — King Charles II grants Connecticut a charter that allows much self-government

1665—Connecticut and New Haven colonies unite

1687—Sir Edmund Andros, royal governor of New York, makes an unsuccessful attempt to take over Connecticut

1701—Collegiate School (now Yale University) is founded

1707—Simsbury Mine, the first American copper mine, begins operation

1740—The first tinware manufacture in the colonies takes place in Berlin

1755—The *Connecticut Gazette*, the first Connecticut newspaper, begins in New Haven

1764—The *Hartford Courant*, the oldest continuously printed newspaper in the United States, begins publication as the *Connecticut Courant*

1765—Connecticut citizens protest the newly passed Stamp Act; Eliphalet Dyer and Jonathan Trumbull form the Sons of Liberty

1773—New-Gate Prison opens in East Granby

1774—Litchfield Law School (later called Tapping Reeve Law School), the first American institution devoted entirely to the teaching of law, opens

1775—Ethan Allen, a native of Litchfield, captures Fort Ticonderoga

1776—Connecticut passes a resolution of independence from Great Britain on June 14; Nathan Hale is executed by the British as a spy

1777—The British burn important colonial supplies stored at Danbury

1779—Israel Putnam drives off British forces at Greenwich

1781—Benedict Arnold, a Connecticut-born soldier who abandoned the colonial army and fought for the British, leads successful attacks on Fort Trumbull and Fort Griswold

1784—A law is passed to free all children born into slavery when they become twenty-five years old

1786—Connecticut cedes its western lands, except for the Western Reserve, to the United States

1787—Delegates from Connecticut propose the Great Compromise that allows large states and small states to agree on a federal constitution

1788—Connecticut ratifies the United States Constitution and enters the Union as the fifth state

1793 — Eli Whitney invents the cotton gin

1794 — The first fire-insurance company opens in Hartford

1795 — Connecticut sells Western Reserve lands for $1.2 million and uses proceeds to establish a school fund

1808 — Eli Terry becomes the first person to make clocks by mass production

1810 — Rodney and Horatio Hanks build the nation's first silk mill, in Mansfield

1814 — The New England Federalists hold the Hartford Convention

1817 — Thomas Hopkins Gallaudet forms the American School for the Deaf

1818 — The Toleration party helps form a new state constitution

1828 — Noah Webster publishes the first American dictionary

1830 — The first industrial union in America, The New England Association of Farmers, Mechanics, and other Workingmen, is organized at Lyme

1833 — Prudence Crandall establishes a short-lived academy for young black women

1836 — Samuel Colt patents the first successful repeating pistol

1839 — Charles Goodyear invents the vulcanization of rubber

1842 — Wadsworth Atheneum, America's oldest public art museum, opens in Hartford

1875 — Connecticut opens the first state agricultural experimental station in the United States

1878 — The first commercial telephone exchange in the world begins in New Haven; the Knights of Labor is organized at New Britain

1881 — Connecticut and New York settle a border dispute, leaving the state with their approximate current boundary

1888 — The Great Blizzard of 1888 kills hundreds of people

1910 — New London becomes the home of the United States Coast Guard Academy

1917 — The United States Navy opens a submarine base in Groton

1936 — A civil-rights law forbids discrimination on the basis of "alienage, color, or race"; Eugene O'Neill receives the Nobel Prize in literature

1943—Connecticut becomes the first state to create a civil-rights commission

1954—The USS *Nautilus*, the first atomic submarine, is launched from Groton

1955—The legislature approves laws giving voters a direct voice in choosing candidates for state elections; severe flooding of Connecticut rivers kills more than one hundred persons

1965—Connecticut adopts its present constitution

1975—Ella Grasso becomes the first woman elected in her own right to assume office as governor of a state

1979—Connecticut adopts a law banning the construction of new nuclear power plants

1981—Thirman L. Milner, elected mayor of Hartford, becomes the first black mayor of a New England city

1990—The state government allocates $2.2 million to Bridgeport's Beardsley Zoo— the only zoo in Connecticut—to build a facsimile of a South American rain forest

IMPORTANT PEOPLE

DEAN ACHESON

Dean Gooderham Acheson (1893-1971), born in Middletown; lawyer and statesman; as U.S. undersecretary of state (1945-47), he was responsible for the Truman Doctrine and helped formulate the Marshall Plan; U.S. secretary of state (1949-53); received the 1970 Pulitzer Prize in history for his book *Present at the Creation: My Years in the State Department*

Ethan Allen (1738-1789), born in Litchfield; soldier; led the Green Mountain Boys in the capture of Fort Ticonderoga (1775)

Benedict Arnold (1741-1801), born in Norwich; soldier; served as an American general before betraying the colonies; later led the British army to victories at Fort Trumbull and Fort Griswold

Phineas Taylor (P. T.) Barnum (1810-1891), born in Bethel; showman; helped found Ringling Brothers Barnum and Bailey Circus; introduced midget Tom Thumb, "Swedish Nightingale" Jenny Lind, and Jumbo the elephant

P. T. BARNUM

CATHARINE BEECHER

HENRY WARD BEECHER

JOHN BROWN

GLENN CLOSE

Catharine Esther Beecher (1800-1878), educator; founded a girls' seminary in Hartford (1823); founded the American Women's Educational Association (1852)

Henry Ward Beecher (1813-1887), born in Litchfield; clergyman; served churches in Indianapolis and Brooklyn; wrote *Aids to Prayer* and *Life of Jesus Christ*

Ed Begley (1901-1970), born in Hartford; actor; versatile star who appeared in thirty-five movies; received the 1962 Academy Award for best supporting actor in *Sweet Bird of Youth*

Hiram Bingham (1875-1956), explorer; discovered Inca ruins at Machu Picchu (1911); governor of Connecticut (1925); U.S. senator (1925-33)

Ernest Borgnine (1919-   ), born in Hamden; actor; received the 1955 Academy Award for best actor for *Marty*; also starred in *The Dirty Dozen* and *Emperor of the North*; portrayed Captain McHale in the television show "McHale's Navy"

Julius Boros (1920-   ), born in Fairfield; professional golfer; known for his long drives; won the 1952 and 1963 U.S. Open and the 1968 PGA championship

John Brown (1800-1859), born in Torrington; abolitionist; fought proslavery forces in Kansas Territory; led a raid on the government arsenal in Harper's Ferry, Virginia, where he was captured; convicted of treason and hanged

Morgan Bulkeley (1837-1922), born in Haddam; businessman, sports executive, politician; first president of baseball's National League (1876); helped Aetna Life become the largest insurance company in the country; governor of Connecticut (1889-93); U.S. senator (1905-11)

Walter Chauncey Camp (1859-1925), born in New Britain; football coach (Yale University, 1888-92); worked to popularize the game of football; originated All-American football selections (1889); became known as the Father of American Football

Al Capp (1909-1979), born Alfred Gabriel Caplin in New Haven; cartoonist; created "L'il Abner" and "Fearless Fosdick"

Karen Carpenter (1950-1982), and **Richard Carpenter** (1946-   ), both born in New Haven; musicians; wrote and performed such songs as "We've Only Just Begun" and "Rainy Days and Mondays"

Lucia Chase (1897-1986), born in Waterbury; ballet dancer; starred in *Petrouchka, Bluebeard*, and *Tally-Ho*; founded Ballet Theatre (now American Ballet Theatre)

Glenn Close (1947-   ), born in Greenwich; actress; appeared in such films as *The World According to Garp, The Big Chill*, and *Fatal Attraction*; won a Tony Award for her role in *The Real Thing* (1984)

Samuel Colt (1814-1862), born in Hartford; inventor; developed the first successful repeating pistol (1836); founded the company that made the Colt .45 revolver

Roger Connor (1857-1931), born in Waterbury; professional baseball player; starred with nineteenth-century New York Giants; elected to the Baseball Hall of Fame in 1976

Prudence Crandall (1803-1890), educator; attempted to establish the first academy for black women in New England, in Canterbury

Jules Dassin (1911-), born in Middletown; motion-picture producer and director; directed *Never On Sunday* and *Topkapi*

Peter de Vries (1910-), author; lives in Westport; his plays and novels poke fun at modern suburban life; wrote *Who Wakes the Bugler?*, *The Handsome Heart*, and *Comfort Me with Apples*

Thomas Dodd (1907-1971), born in Norwich; politician; assistant to the U.S. attorney general (1938-45); helped create the first civil-rights section in the Justice Department; U.S. representative (1953-57); U.S. senator (1959-71); led the fight for gun control

George Henry Durrie (1820-1863); artist; painted many Connecticut landscapes that later became Currier and Ives prints; painted *Home for Thanksgiving*

Jonathan Edwards (1703-1757), born in East Windsor; clergyman; became a leading intellectual figure of the early colonial years; wrote sermons that led to the colonial religious revival known as the Great Awakening

Oliver Ellsworth (1745-1807), born in Windsor; politician, jurist; served in the Continental Congress (1777-84) and Constitutional Convention (1787); played a leading role in establishing the federal judiciary system; chief justice of the U.S. Supreme Court (1796-1800)

Linda Evans (1942-), born in Hartford; actress; starred in such television shows as "The Big Valley" and "Dynasty"

Eileen Farrell (1920-), born in Willimantic; opera singer; starred in "Eileen Farrell Sings," a 1940s radio show; starred in such operas as *La Gioconda*, *Medea*, and *Il Trovatore*

Stephen Field (1816-1899), born in Haddam; jurist; associate justice of the U.S. Supreme Court (1863-97); wrote many opinions that helped develop constitutional law

Thomas Hopkins Gallaudet (1783-1851), educator; founded the first free school for the deaf in America at Hartford (1817)

William Hooker Gillette (1855-1937), born in Hartford; playwright and actor; became known for plays rich with swift-moving action and detail; wrote *Esmeralda* and *Mr. Wilkerson's Widows*; won fame for his portrayal of Sherlock Holmes

SAMUEL COLT

THOMAS DODD

EILEEN FARRELL

WILLIAM GILLETTE

CHARLES GOODYEAR

KATHARINE HEPBURN

GORDIE HOWE

EDWARD KENDALL

Charles Goodyear (1800-1860), born in New Haven; inventor; created the vulcanizing process (1839), which keeps rubber from melting in heat

Ella Grasso (1919-1981), born in Windsor Locks; politician; Connecticut secretary of state (1958-70); the first woman to be elected governor who did not succeed her husband in office (1975-81)

Nathan Hale (1755-1776), born in Coventry; teacher and patriot; served as a spy for American forces (1776); was captured and hanged by the British; became famous for his last words, "I only regret that I have but one life to lose for my country"

Katharine Hepburn (1909-   ), born in Hartford; actress; received nominations for a record twelve Academy Awards; won a record four Academy Awards for best actress; starred in *Guess Who's Coming to Dinner, The Lion in Winter,* and *On Golden Pond,* among many other movies

Thomas Hooker (1586-1647), clergyman; exerted strong influence in drafting the Fundamental Orders of 1639; became the political and spiritual leader of the Connecticut Colony

Gordie Howe (1928-   ), professional hockey player; scored more goals and more points than any other National Hockey League player; concluded his playing career as the star of the Hartford Whalers (1977-78); Whalers executive (1982-   )

Isaac Hull (1773-1843), born in Derby; naval officer; commanded the USS *Constitution* ("Old Ironsides"); defeated the British ship *Guerrière* in the War of 1812

Collis P. Huntington (1821-1900), born in Farmington; financier, railroad builder; promoted building the western section of the transcontinental railroad (1861-69); helped create the Southern Pacific Railroad (1884)

Charles Edward Ives (1874-1954), born in Danbury; composer; was considered among the most original of American composers; wrote more than 150 songs and choral works; received the 1947 Pulitzer Prize in music for Symphony No. 3

Edward Calvin Kendall (1886-1972), born in Norwalk; scientist; shared the 1950 Nobel Prize in medicine for his work on the hormone ACTH

John Frederick Kensett (1816-1872), born in Cheshire; artist; gained renown as one of the leading landscape painters of the nineteenth-century Hudson River school; painted scenes of the Great Lakes and the Hudson River

Ted Knight (1923-1986), born Tadeus Wladyslaw Konopka in Terryville; actor; won Emmy awards for his portrayal of bumbling newscaster Ted Baxter in the television series "The Mary Tyler Moore Show"

Norman Lear (1922-   ), born in New Haven; television producer; created controversial and relevant television series such as "All in the Family," "Maude," and "The Jeffersons"

Clare Booth Luce (1903-1987), playwright, politician, and diplomat; wrote *Abide with Me* and *Margin for Error*; elected from Connecticut to U.S. House of Representatives (1943-47); U.S. ambassador to Italy (1953-56)

CLARE BOOTH LUCE

Roger Ludlow (1590?-1664), magistrate; helped found the Connecticut Colony (1636); presided over the first court held in Connecticut (1636); collected and codified Connecticut's laws (1650)

Barbara McClintock (1902-   ), born in Hartford; biologist; received the 1983 Nobel Prize in medicine for her discovery that genes can change their position in chromosomes

Robert Mitchum (1917-   ), born in Bridgeport; actor; starred in "he-man" roles in *Night of the Hunter, The Sundowners,* and *The Winds of War*

BARBARA McCLINTOCK

John Pierpont (J. P.) Morgan (1837-1913), born in Hartford; financier; helped organize the U.S. Steel Corp., International Harvester, American Telephone and Telegraph, and General Electric; reorganized the Northern Pacific, Erie, and Southern railroads; donated many valuable paintings, sculptures, and books to libraries and museums

Calvin Murphy (1948-   ), born in Norwalk; professional basketball player; starred with the Houston Rockets; earned recognition for his great free-throw shooting

CALVIN MURPHY

George Murphy (1902-   ), born in New Haven; actor and politician; sang and danced in such films as *I'll Love You Always* and *Broadway Melody of 1938*; U.S. senator from California (1965-71)

Ralph Nader (1934-   ), born in Winsted; consumer advocate; fought business and government interests and the automobile, coal, meat, and other industries; wrote *Unsafe at Any Speed* and *Who Runs Congress?*

Frederick Law Olmsted (1822-1903), born in Hartford; landscape architect; designed New York City's Central Park, Chicago's Columbian Exposition, and the U.S. Capitol grounds

Eugene Gladstone O'Neill (1888-1953), playwright; spent boyhood summers in New London; earned fame for his tragic plays; received the 1936 Nobel Prize in literature; received Pulitzer Prizes in drama for *Beyond the Horizon* (1920), *Anna Christie* (1922), *Strange Interlude* (1928), and *Long Day's Journey into Night* (1957)

RALPH NADER

ROSA PONSELLE

ROGER SHERMAN

JOHN SIRICA

BENJAMIN SPOCK

James "Orator Jim" O'Rourke (1852-1919), born in East Bridgeport; professional baseball player; got the first hit in National League history; starred with Boston, Providence, and New York teams; elected to the Baseball Hall of Fame in 1945

Rosa Ponselle (1897-1981), born in Meriden; operatic soprano; gained renown for the richness and tone of her voice; appeared with the New York Metropolitan Opera (1918-36) in *Don Giovanni, Norma, La Gioconda,* and *Aida*

Israel Putnam (1718-1790), farmer and soldier; had a farm in Pomfret; served in the French and Indian War (1756-63); appointed major general in the Continental army; shouted "Don't fire until you see the whites of their eyes!" at the Battle of Bunker Hill

Tapping Reeve (1744-1823), educator, jurist; founded Litchfield Law School, the first law school in America (1774); Connecticut Superior Court judge (1798-1814); started a movement to give women equal rights over property

Abraham Ribicoff (1910-   ), born in New Britain; politician; U.S. representative (1949-53); governor of Connecticut (1955-61); secretary of the U.S. Department of Health, Education, and Welfare (1961-62); U.S. senator (1963-81); led the fight for safety features in automobiles

Rosalind Russell (1912-1976), born in Waterbury; actress; portrayed bold, independent working women; received Oscar nominations for her work in *My Sister Eileen, Auntie Mame, Mourning Becomes Electra,* and *Picnic*

Roger Sherman (1721-1793), statesman; was the only person to sign all four of the following documents: the Articles of Association, the Declaration of Independence, the Articles of Confederation, and the U.S. Constitution; presented the Connecticut Compromise to settle the disagreement between the large states and the small states at the Constitutional Convention; U.S. representative (1789-91); U.S. senator (1791-93)

Igor Sikorsky (1889-1972), engineer; pioneered the design of helicopters and multiengine airplanes at his Hartford company (today called United Technologies)

John J. Sirica (1904-   ), born in Waterbury; jurist; presided over the Watergate break-in trial and subsequent related trials; demanded and received presidential tapes from President Richard M. Nixon

Benjamin Spock (1903-   ), born in New Haven; physician, educator; wrote the best-selling nonfiction book of all time, *Baby and Child Care*; led opposition to U.S. involvement in the Vietnam War

Harriet Beecher Stowe (1811-1896), born in Litchfield; author; wrote the famed antislavery book *Uncle Tom's Cabin*

John Trumbull (1756-1843), born in Lebanon; artist; depicted the American Revolution in many small, dramatic paintings such as *Battle of Bunker's Hill* and *The Signing of the Declaration of Independence*

Jonathan Trumbull (1710-1785), born in Lebanon; politician; founded the Sons of Liberty; governor (1776-84); supported the Continental army with food and ammunition

Thomas Tryon (1926-   ), born in Hartford; actor and author; starred in many Shakespearean plays and in the movie *The Cardinal*; wrote *The Other*

Mark Twain (1835-1910), born Samuel Langhorne Clemens; author and humorist; his books *Life on the Mississippi, A Connecticut Yankee in King Arthur's Court, The Adventures of Tom Sawyer,* and *Adventures of Huckleberry Finn* were written in Hartford

Uncas (1588?-1683?), chief of the Mohegan Indians; aided and corresponded with the English settlers; sided with the colonists in their war against the Pequots; served as the model for "Uncas" in James Fenimore Cooper's book *Last of the Mohicans*

Noah Webster (1758-1843), born in Hartford; lexicographer, author; compiled the first major American dictionary; wrote spelling and history textbooks

Lowell Palmer Weicker, Jr. (1931-   ), politician; elected from Connecticut to U.S. House of Representatives (1969-71) and U.S. Senate (1971-89); gained nationwide fame for his opposition to the Nixon administration when he served on the Senate Watergate Committee (1973-74)

George Weiss (1894-1972), born in New Haven; baseball executive; led the New York Yankees to ten pennants in twelve years as general manager; elected to the Baseball Hall of Fame in 1971

Gideon Welles (1802-1878), born in Glastonbury; politician; organized the Union blockade of Confederate ports while secretary of the navy (1861-69); upheld the Reconstruction policy of President Andrew Johnson

Eli Whitney (1765-1825), inventor; graduate of Yale University; built the first cotton gin (1793); created standardized parts for guns; operated a firearms factory in Whitneyville

Emma Willard (1787-1870), born in Berlin; educator and author; wrote poems and history textbooks; founded schools for young women in Connecticut and New York; opened the way for women's high schools and colleges

Elihu Yale (1649-1721), English philanthropist; donated books and other valuable items to the Collegiate School of Connecticut, which was renamed Yale University in his honor

JONATHAN TRUMBULL

ELI WHITNEY

EMMA WILLARD

ELIHU YALE

GOVERNORS

Jonathan Trumbull	1776-1784	Phineas C. Lounsbury	1887-1889
Matthew Griswold	1784-1786	Morgan G. Bulkeley	1889-1893
Samuel Huntington	1786-1796	Luzon B. Morris	1893-1895
Oliver Wolcott	1796-1797	O. Vincent Coffin	1895-1897
Jonathan Trumbull II	1797-1809	Lorrin A. Cooke	1897-1899
John Treadwell	1809-1811	George E. Lounsbury	1899-1901
Roger Griswold	1811-1812	George P. McLean	1901-1903
John Cotton Smith	1812-1817	Abiram Chamberlain	1903-1905
Oliver Wolcott, Jr.	1817-1827	Henry Roberts	1905-1907
Gideon Tomlinson	1827-1831	Rollin S. Woodruff	1907-1909
John S. Peters	1831-1833	George L. Lilley	1909
Henry W. Edwards	1833-1834	Frank B. Weeks	1909-1911
Samuel A. Foot	1834-1835	Simeon E. Baldwin	1911-1915
Henry W. Edwards	1835-1838	Marcus H. Holcomb	1915-1921
William W. Ellsworth	1838-1842	Everett J. Lake	1921-1923
Chauncey F. Cleveland	1842-1844	Charles A. Templeton	1923-1925
Roger S. Baldwin	1844-1846	Hiram Bingham	1925
Isaac Toucey	1846-1847	John H. Trumbull	1925-1931
Clark Bissell	1847-1849	Wilbur L. Cross	1931-1939
Joseph Trumbull	1849-1850	Raymond E. Baldwin	1939-1941
Thomas H. Seymour	1850-1853	Robert A. Hurley	1941-1943
Charles H. Pond	1853-1854	Raymond E. Baldwin	1943-1946
Henry Dutton	1854-1855	Wilbert Snow	1946-1947
William T. Minor	1855-1857	James L. McConaughy	1947-1948
Alexander H. Holley	1857-1858	James C. Shannon	1948-1949
William A. Buckingham	1858-1866	Chester Bowles	1949-1951
Joseph R. Hawley	1866-1867	John Lodge	1951-1955
James E. English	1867-1869	Abraham A. Ribicoff	1955-1961
Marshall Jewell	1869-1870	John N. Dempsey	1961-1971
James E. English	1870-1871	Thomas J. Meskill	1971-1975
Marshall Jewell	1871-1873	Ella T. Grasso	1975-1981
Charles R. Ingersoll	1873-1877	William A. O'Neill	1981-
Richard D. Hubbard	1877-1879		
Charles B. Andrews	1879-1881		
Hobart B. Bigelow	1881-1883		
Thomas M. Waller	1883-1885		
Henry B. Harrison	1885-1887		

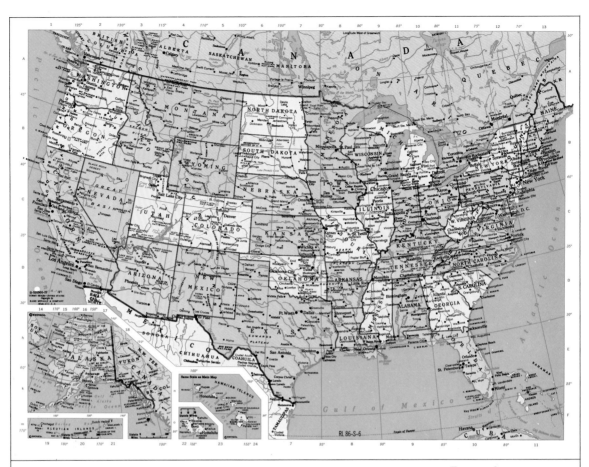

RL 86-S-6

Topography

| 5,000 m. 16,404 ft. | 2,000 m. 6,562 ft. | 1,000 m. 3,281 ft. | 500 m. 1,640 ft. | 200 m. 656 ft. | 100 m. 328 ft. | Sea Level | Below |

135

Lambert Conformal Conic Projection

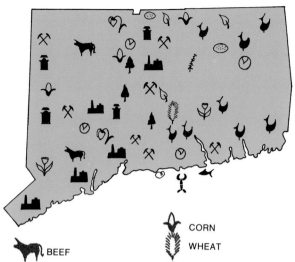

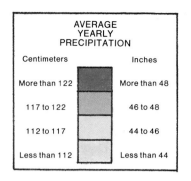

AVERAGE YEARLY PRECIPITATION

Centimeters		Inches
More than 122		More than 48
117 to 122		46 to 48
112 to 117		44 to 46
Less than 112		Less than 44

BEEF

POULTRY

DAIRY PRODUCTS

POTATOES

VEGETABLES

NURSERY PRODUCTS

TOBACCO

OATS

CORN

WHEAT

FRUIT

BERRIES

MINING

MANUFACTURING

OYSTERS

FISH

LOBSTERS

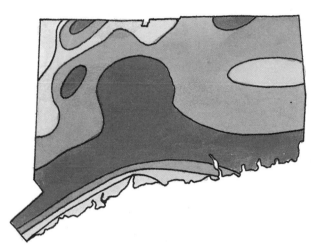

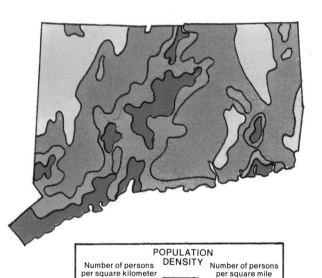

POPULATION DENSITY

Number of persons per square kilometer		Number of persons per square mile
More than 400		More than 1,000
200 to 400		500 to 1,000
40 to 200		100 to 500
Less than 40		Less than 100

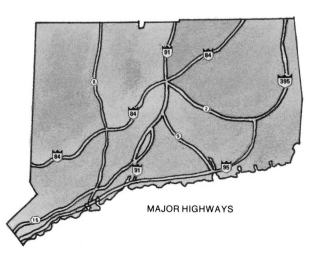

MAJOR HIGHWAYS

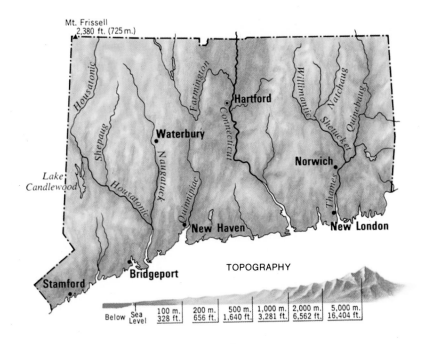

Mt. Frissell
2,380 ft. (725 m.)

Housatonic

Shepaug

Lake
Candlewood

Housatonic

Naugatuck

Waterbury

Quinipiac

Farmington

Connecticut

Hartford

Willimantic

Natchaug

Shetucket

Quinebaug

Norwich

Thames

New London

New Haven

Stamford

Bridgeport

TOPOGRAPHY

| Below Sea Level | 100 m. 328 ft. | 200 m. 656 ft. | 500 m. 1,640 ft. | 1,000 m. 3,281 ft. | 2,000 m. 6,562 ft. | 5,000 m. 16,404 ft. |

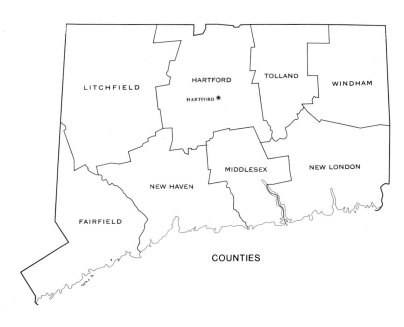

LITCHFIELD

HARTFORD

HARTFORD ✳

TOLLAND

WINDHAM

NEW HAVEN

MIDDLESEX

NEW LONDON

FAIRFIELD

COUNTIES

Autumn on a rural Connecticut road

INDEX

Page numbers that appear in boldface type indicate illustrations

Shops and restaurants line a brick sidewalk in historic South Norwalk.

Picture Identifications

Front Cover: Mystic Seaport
Back Cover: A Lakeville scene
Pages 2-3: A sunset at Lighthouse Point, New Haven
Page 6: First Congregational Church, Litchfield
Pages 8-9: The town of Mystic
Pages 18-19: Montage of Connecticut residents
Pages 24-25: *Hooker and Company Journeying through the Wilderness from Plymouth to Hartford in 1636*, an 1846 Frederic Edwin Church painting of Thomas Hooker's party
Pages 42-43: The Hitchcock Chair Factory, in Riverton, which was established in 1826 and is still in use
Page 58: Occupants of the reviewing stand observe the 1935 parade commemorating the three-hundredth birthday of Connecticut
Pages 68-69: The state capitol, Hartford
Pages 78-79: The Goodspeed Opera House, in East Haddam
Pages 90-91: An autumn view of Nash's Pond, in Westport
Page 108: A montage of the state flag, the state tree (white oak), the state bird (robin), and the state flower (mountain laurel)

About the Author

Deborah Kent grew up in Little Falls, New Jersey. She received a Bachelor of Arts degree in English from Oberlin College and a Master's Degree from Smith College School for Social Work. After spending four years as a social worker in New York City, she moved to San Miguel de Allende, Mexico, where she began to write full-time.

Deborah Kent is the author of several novels for young adults as well as many books in the *America the Beautiful* series. She lives in Chicago with her husband and their daughter Janna.

Picture Acknowledgments